Creative Practice and Socioeconomic Crisis in the Caribbean

Although the world is saturated with extraordinary methods, innovation, and technology, the Caribbean seems to have been left behind in the sustainable growth of global development. While the majority of the world defines the Caribbean as "paradise," the reality of life for Afro-Caribbean culture is defined by an unrelenting hardship. This book comprehensively analyzes this phenomenon from a unique and intimate perspective in order to offer a viable pathway to sustainable growth.

By examining the historic progression of the Caribbean region and the African culture within, the author explores the relationship between creative practice and socioeconomic crisis and questions whether limited access to environments that facilitate original and conceptual ideas correlates with socioeconomic crisis. The outcomes and methods of analysis developed in this book are a useful tool for other cultures or organizations seeking to diffuse socioeconomic crisis and implement a pathway of sustainable growth.

This innovative book will be of great interest to students and scholars of cultural and sustainability studies, Caribbean and African Studies, as well as Development and Sustainable Development.

Kent J. Wessinger holds an earned PhD in Sustainability Education with a research emphasis in creative practice as a path to sustainable growth. Kent founded the create2elevate foundation in 2015.

Creative Practice and Socioeconomic Crisis in the Caribbean

A Path to Sustainable Growth

Kent J. Wessinger

LONDON AND NEW YORK

from Routledge

First published 2017
by Routledge

2 Park Square, Milton Park, Abingdon, Oxfordshire OX14 4RN
52 Vanderbilt Avenue, New York, NY 10017

Routledge is an imprint of the Taylor & Francis Group, an informa business

First issued in paperback 2018

British Library Cataloguing-in-Publication Data
A catalogue record for this book is available from the British Library

Library of Congress Cataloging-in-Publication Data
A catalog record for this book has been requested

ISBN: 978-0-415-78442-9 (hbk)
ISBN: 978-0-367-14531-6 (pbk)

Typeset in Bembo
by Wearset Ltd, Boldon, Tyne and Wear

To future generations of creative practitioners
in the Caribbean

Contents

4   An intentional reality: three lenses of perspective   49

5   Amplifying the Afro-Carib voice—research design and
       methodology   91

6   Emergent themes—participant generated findings   108

Figures

Tables

Acknowledgments

Jamaica & St. John, USVI—thank you for loving me and my children as one of you.

West Indian/Afro-Carib culture—we remain forever bound in friendship, sacrifice, and respect.

Four years prior to the publication of this research project, all three of my children freely agreed to support, encourage, and inspire me to elevate the region we call home—thank you Carson, Maggie, and Sam Wessinger.

I could not have completed this project without the support and love of Laurie Wessinger.

Mom and Paul—thank you for not giving up on me or my passion for the Caribbean.

Dad—you would have been proud.

Pramod Parajuli—you inspired me to embrace a depth of understanding that I have never experienced, thank you for your leadership and guidance. I will not let you down.

Mark Runco—your perspective of creativity has motivated people to engage in practice all around the world, maybe none more than me. Thank you.

Roy Beckford—our paths have crossed for a divine purpose.

Jaco Maree—thank you for the model of authentic relationship.

1 An intentional task—motivated by hardship and respect

A debilitating phenomenon has been escalating throughout the Caribbean for five centuries—while the majority of the world defines the Caribbean as "paradise," the reality of life for the Afro-Carib culture is defined by an unrelenting hardship.[1] This project comprehensively analyzes the phenomenon and offers a viable path to sustainable growth.

I have experienced the reality of island life in the Caribbean from multiple cultural perspectives. Based on nearly two decades of experiences, two key themes seem to define the region: (a) due to a perpetual socioeconomic crisis, hardship has become an accepted way of life, and (b) surviving the hardship requires a raw creative effort to complete the simplest of tasks. After many years of observing the culture suffer through escalating hardship, I still hear the same repetitive question in reference to the reality of life in the Caribbean, "Why is this hardship happening to us?" Although the world is saturated with extraordinary methods, innovation, and technology, the Caribbean seems to have been left behind or not included in global development. Thus, the motivation for this project is steeped in animosity for unjust hardship, profound respect for the plight, and sincere affection for the cultures in the Caribbean.

Positionality disclosure

My positionality is significant and relative to the process and outcomes of this project since the "critical ethnographer contributes to emancipatory knowledge and discourses of social justice" (as cited in Madison, 2012, p. 6).[2] Therefore, in an effort to be transparent, it seems ethically imperative to fully disclose my positionality as a participant and observer in the Caribbean.

The occupational positions I have been honored to hold in the Caribbean include, but are not limited to, the following: first, headmaster of a residential academic/vocational school in rural Jamaica. The student body at the school was comprised of young men, between the ages of fifteen and nineteen years old, who did not meet the criteria to attend a government high school. Second, founder of two university satellite campuses in the British Virgin Islands and St. Kitts. Third, an honors teacher at a private high school on St.

John, United States Virgin Islands. Fourth, as an instructor of mathematics and philosophy at the University of the Virgin Islands on St. Thomas, U.S. Virgin Islands and the program director of a satellite campus on St. John, U.S. Virgin Islands. As a resident of four distinctly different islands, visits to nineteen other islands in the region, and an active participant in the reality of Caribbean life, I am passionately motivated to understand "why" the Caribbean cultures are suffering through long-standing and escalating socioeconomic crisis. Yet, the ultimate objective of this project is to reach beyond "why" and illuminate "how" sustainable growth for the cultures can be an active reality.

Positioned as a participant and observer

I have witnessed socioeconomic hardship throughout the Caribbean despite billions of tourist dollars expended and invested in the respective economies. From my house in rural Jamaica, the rusted ruins of a closed bauxite plant laid in full view in the valley below, a reflection of how errant decisions derailed growth in the past. I have observed the region transition from a pure food source to a mass importer of processed and genetically modified foods. I personally know business owners who were forced to close their businesses due to exorbitant energy costs, which is the result of the region's dependency on fossil fuels. For over a decade, while living in the U.S. Virgin Islands, I paid the highest electricity rate in the world at fifty-two cents per kilowatt (U.S. Energy Information Administration, 2016). Due to the state of the economies and excessive high costs of living, I know upstanding people who have reverted to illegal activity in order to survive. As a result of a desperate atmosphere throughout the Caribbean, I have been a victim and observer of horrendous crimes in the region.

Over the course of two decades in the region, I have witnessed friends, co-workers, and many others migrate to the United States, Canada, and Western Europe. Due to the influence of expatriates elevating housing costs in the region, I have observed the rapid demise of a culture that can no longer afford to live on the island of their birth. I have watched children grow through adolescence with very little organized extracurricular activity, educational facilities in need of substantial renovation, and a high percentage of absentee fathers. I have witnessed emotional breakdowns from grandparents, parents, and students over the lack of educational opportunities.

As an observer, I watched developers build expatriates exclusive second homes, while leaving no green space on the building lot. I have witnessed coconut trees, palm trees, and mangroves on the beaches cut down to construct temporary tourist traps; while the beaches slowly dissipate into the sea. I have observed the influence of European and American culture dominate and dismantle the Afro-Carib culture.[3] The overwhelming majority of my observations suggest that there is a high level of desperation that motivates significant decisions throughout the Caribbean.

Yet, through all the observed hardship, life in the Caribbean has also allowed me to develop the most meaningful relationships in my life. Although it seems that much of the world falsely views the Afro-Carib culture through a non-productive lens of drugs and beach bars, I discovered a highly relational culture that is steeped in substance. Those relationships have provided me with a life perspective that looks beyond convenience, entitlement, and the subtlety of first world materialism—relationships that fully embrace the depth and meaning of a lifetime bond.

Based on my observations, the reality of everyday life for the Caribbean cultures requires creative survival skills. I have witnessed individuals create water catchments in the dry season, construct forms of transportation that are not acceptable in other parts of the world, and develop alternative cooking methods that efficiently produce culinary excellence. Due to the costs and difficulty of acquiring materials, no facet of life is exempt from using the waste from another area of life in an effort to remain semi-functional. The cultures depend on creativity for survival; however, as a participant and observer, the Caribbean cultures are longing for more than a protracted state of survival; there is a broad and passionate desire to experience stability and growth.

Project overview

This project will explicitly focus on the relationship between creative practice and the socioeconomic crisis within the African cultures in the Caribbean.[4] Acknowledging that nearly forty million people from diverse cultural backgrounds live in the region, I recognize that the scale and scope of this project must contain clear lines of delineation in order to produce effective outcomes (Table 1.1). In order to achieve the highest level of effectiveness for the people of the Caribbean, this project has been segmented into five distinct modules—my positionality, an historical progression of the region, multidisciplinary theoretical positions, methodology for conducting respectful and thorough research, and the voice of the African culture in the Caribbean. The summation of this project will analyze similar and consistent themes that emerge from each of the modules. The comprehensive analysis of those themes will be utilized to develop a pathway of sustainable growth for all those who call the Caribbean "home."

First, I begin the project by establishing my magnified positionality within the context of the project. Nine experiences, which I term Magnified Moments, are employed to elucidate the socioeconomic crisis that exists in the Caribbean. I begin with these rich descriptions because I am sensitive to the biases of researchers who are not members of the culture they are researching. The Magnified Moments reveal my authentic appreciation and understanding for the reality of life on islands throughout the Caribbean. These moments are important to this project because they establish my credibility as a voice within the culture and an experiential participant in the plight of the African people in the Caribbean. They also expose the motivation that fuels my intellectual pursuit of understanding the relationship that exists between creative practice and the socioeconomic crisis in the Caribbean.

Next, I provide a *historical progression* of the Caribbean—"Paradise" lost in crisis. The objective of this section is to describe the plight of the African culture in the Caribbean through a historical progression. The five historical periods/phases reflect over 500 years of Caribbean history. Each of the periods—encounter, colonial, decolonization, developmental, and neo-liberal—represents an ontological perspective that provide significant understanding into creative practice and socioeconomic crisis within the African culture in the Caribbean.

In the third section of the project, I provide three theoretical lenses to examine *why* the African culture in the Caribbean continues to suffer through long-term socioeconomic crisis and *how* creative practice relates to the crisis. To establish a relevant pathway of understanding, the three theoretical lenses are developed through two perspectives: (1) African scholars in the Caribbean; and (2) scholars outside the region who speak directly to the respective lenses in the Caribbean. Each lens is sub-sectioned into positions that substantiate theoretical rationale and clarity to the relationship between creative practice and socioeconomic crisis.

Fourth, I describe the *research design and methodology*. Designed within distinct boundaries, this project utilizes a qualitative structure with a transformative phenomenological methodology to comprehensively analyze the relationship between creative practice and socioeconomic crisis in the Caribbean. The need for regional transformation, longstanding crisis, and the suppression of creative practice are the phenomena that justify utilizing the principles of the transformative phenomenology research model.

Last, the voice of the people is essential to the validity and outcomes of this project. Therefore, the highest priority has been given to the African culture on St. John, United States Virgin Islands. Capturing the Afro-Carib voice depicts the reality of everyday life in the Caribbean from a firsthand point of view. To comprehensively capture the voice, I conducted one-on-one conversational interviews with six diverse demographics within the Afro-Carib community.

The outcomes of this project should produce relevant information that clarifies the relationship between creative practice and socioeconomic crisis. Since the outcomes could have significant long-term influence in the region, it seems imperative that the boundaries of research be clearly delineated (Figure 1.1) and the process defined (Table 1.1).

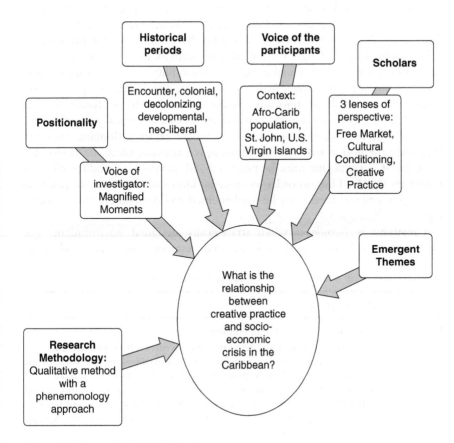

Figure 1.1 Research design/objective.

Foresight—clarifying "intentional creative practice"

Opportunities only exist once they have been seen. And they will only be seen if they are looked for.

(de Bono, 1992)

Recognizing that ambiguity impedes process, reduces the probability of effective outcomes, and fortifies the status quo; this project utilizes a collective point of understanding to clarify "intentional creative practice." Runco's research and applied experience suggests that creativity is defined as "Vital originality balanced with fit and appropriateness" (1988, p. 4). Csikszentmihalyl states, "Creativity can be defined as an idea or product that is original, valued and implemented" (1996, p. 28). Ken Robinson defines creativity as, "the process of having original ideas that have value" (2006).

Imbedded in each of the perspectives are traits that suggest that creativity is dependent upon "originality and effectiveness" (Runco & Jaeger, 2012, p. 2). Since *originality and effectiveness* are not mutually exclusive to intentionality, I acknowledge that seemingly random acts of creativity have produced products or solutions that have advanced the global community. A few examples would be the pacemaker, dynamite, Velcro, anesthesia, and Viagra (Rogers, 2006). Although each of those innovative advancements has been characterized as accidents, they were developed in environments that strategically facilitated *original and effective* ideas—an environment where creative thinking abounds. Rejecting the notion that creative thinking is a mystical talent, de Bono suggests that it is a skill that must be practiced and nurtured to produce effective outcomes (1992). Thus, in order to move an individual or culture beyond the status quo, original ideas must be implemented and deemed effective through a process of intentional creative practice.

Creativity is *intentional* when strategically designed environments can be accessed to develop original ideas, attain effective outcomes, and refine

Table 1.1 Research: what the reader should and should not expect

	Project expectations
Present	The utmost respect for all cultures.
	The development of the relationship between creative practice and socioeconomic crisis through theoretical perspectives, the voice of the people, historical analysis, and the positionality of the investigator.
	Theoretical positions that substantiate the basis for, current status of, and the plight deriving from the socioeconomic crisis in the Caribbean.
	The representation of the reality of life through the voice of the African culture in the Caribbean.
	St. John, United States Virgin Islands, serves as a point of reference for the entire region.
	Statistical data that supports the socioeconomic crisis in the region.
	A historical summary of the region that substantiates the current socioeconomic crisis.
	The essential role of creative practice as a sustainable response to socioeconomic crisis in the Caribbean.
	Data that supports a sustainable response to the socioeconomic crisis in the Caribbean based on the findings in St. John, United States Virgin Islands.
Not present	A concise assessment of the Spanish, French and Dutch islands in the Caribbean.
	A cultural assessment that extends beyond the African culture in the Caribbean.
	An over-reaching analysis into the regions that border the Caribbean Sea (Caribbean Basin).
	A thorough scientific ecological analysis of the region or Virgin Islands
	A "one size fits all" assessment of the region and its crisis points.

processes of implementation.[5] *Practice* specifically refers to the type of activity within the environment—i.e., shaping and re-shaping a conceptual idea into an implemented reality through the access of tools, facilities, and instruction (Runco, 2014). Thus, the objective of this project is to determine if *intentional creative practice* is a viable and sustainable solution to the socioeconomic crisis in the Caribbean.

Notes

1 In the context of this project Afro-Caribs, West Indians, and Africans in the Caribbean, are the same people/culture. Although the term West Indian currently refers directly to the Africans in the Caribbean, it should be noted that West Indians may not be exclusively of African descent. The term West Indian is the result of Columbus' error. When he landed in the Caribbean in 1492, he thought he was in the Indies (Asia), which is east. When the mistake was realized, the term West Indies was used to describe the region. However, the transatlantic slave trade did not develop until a century after Columbus arrived in the Caribbean. When the Africans were violently extracted from their homeland and relocated to the Caribbean, they were designated as West Indians. Due to intercultural relations, rape of female slaves throughout the imperialistic age, and the rise of European populations in the Caribbean, many West Indians have genealogical roots in Africa, Europe, and Asia.
2 A critical ethnographer observes and explores cultural phenomena as subjects in the respective research project.
3 Afro-Carib: Africans in the Caribbean. Reference Glossary A.
4 In this section and subsequent sections the terms, "creative" and "practice" will be defined and clarified.
5 An example of intentional creative practice would be Lego's schools of innovation—

> *Discovering how real-world technology and engineering works.* LEGO Education Machines & Mechanisms gives you the tools and activities to teach about real-world technology and engineering problems and solutions. Build and explore machines and mechanisms, investigate motorized machines, capture wind and study gearing mechanisms. This range of tools takes the learning out of the books and places it directly in the hands of students. We help you get started quickly with easy-to-use activities, guidance and real-world inspiration that bridges technology and science textbooks.
>
> (www.education.lego.com, February 2016)

References

Capra, F. (2002). *The hidden connections: Integrating the biological, cognitive, and social dimensions of life into a science of sustainability.* New York, NY: Doubleday.

Capra, F., & Luisi, P. (2014). *The systems view of life: A unifying vision.* Cambridge: Cambridge University Press.

Creswell, J. (2007). *Qualitative inquiry & research design: Choosing among five approaches.* London: Sage Publications.

Creswell, J. (2013). *Qualitative inquiry & research design: Choosing among five approaches* (2nd ed.). London: Sage Publications.

Csikszentmihalyl, M. (1996). *Creativity: Flow and the psychology of discovery and invention* (1st ed.). New York, NY: HarperCollins.

de Bono, E. (1992). *Opportunities*. Westminster, U.K.: Penguin Books.

Focus-Migration (2016, January). Retrieved from www.focus-migration.hwwi.de

Girvan, N., & Girvan C. (1973). The development of dependency economics in the Caribbean and Latin America: Review and comparison. *Social and Economic Studies*, 22(1): 1–33. Retrieved from http://sesjournaluwi.blogspot.com

Girvan, N. (2007, July). Towards a single development vision and the role of the single economy, presented at the Twenty-Eighth Meeting of the Conference of Heads of Government on the Caribbean Community, Needham's Point, Barbados.

Girvan, N. (2012, November). Colonialism and neo-colonialism in the Caribbean: An overview. Paper presented at the IV International Seminar Africa, the Caribbean, and Latin America, Kingston, Jamaica. Retrieved from www.normangirvan. info/wp-content/uploads/2013/01/Girvan-St-Vincent-paper.pdf

International Monetary Fund (2012, April 12). *World economic outlook: Western hemisphere, rebuilding strength and flexibility*. Retrieved from www.imf.org/external/pubs/ft/reo/2012/whd/eng/pdf/wreo0412.pdf

About the global peace index. (2013). *Vision of humanity*. Retrieved from www. visionofhumanity.org/#/page/about-gpi

Madison, S. (2012). *Critical ethnography: Method, ethics, and performance*. London: Sage Publications.

Robinson, K. (2006, February). How schools kill creativity. *TED*. Retrieved from www.ted.com/talks/ken_robinson_says_schools_kill_creativity?language=en

Rodney, W. (1972). *How Europe underdeveloped Africa*. Baltimore, MD: Black Classic Press (original work published 1972).

Rogers, F. (2006, October). *Ethics of Invention*. Retrieved from www.baylor.edu/content/services/document.php/39555.pdf

Runco, M. (2014). *Creativity: Theories and themes: Research, development, and practice*. London: Academic Press.

Runco, M., & Jaeger, G. (2012). The Standard Definition of Creativity. *Creative Research Journal*, 24(1): 92–96.

Runco, M. A. (1988). Creativity research: Originality, utility, and integration. *Creativity Research Journal*, 1(1): 1–7.

U.S. Energy Information Administration. (2016, October). U.S. Virgin Islands territory energy profile. Retrieved from www.eia.gov/state/print.cfm?sid=VQ

World Bank Group. (2015). *The world bank*. Retrieved from www.worldbank.org

2   A participant in crisis—magnified positionality

Recognizing that I bring biases and values that reflect the Afro-Carib culture into this project, it is essential that my positionality be fully exposed (Creswell, 1998). Although my position in the Afro-Carib community is firmly established in the Magnified Moments in this chapter, my observations as a participant in the socioeconomic crisis in the Caribbean will be utilized as a point of contrast or confirmation throughout this project. Thus, the structure of this project is not random; it was developed through personal experiences and authentic concern for the current and future realities regarding the cultures in the Caribbean.

Cultural tourism: not me

As a resident in the Caribbean for nearly two decades, I have observed a phenomenon that I define as cultural tourism. From my perspective, cultural tourists visit the Caribbean for their yearly holiday and immediately become enamored with the aquamarine waters, volcanic mountains, and tropical foliage. After a visit to a seaside bar, hearing Bob Marley's "Songs of Freedom," and eating fresh lobster on the beach, they are convinced that island life is their foremost destiny. Searching for justification to relocate to "paradise," they observe dark skinned children and judge them as poor and in need of assistance. Having viewed the situation through their lenses of socioeconomic stability, a self-induced "epiphany" convinces them that they possess unique knowledge that will eradicate the island of its longstanding hardship.

Fittingly, the outcomes are not pleasant for many cultural tourists who relocate to "paradise" to satisfy their self-induced epiphanies. They often leave the region after offending the culture with their "first world" absolutes—"Your schools are not structured correctly, your businesses are out of order, and your government is dysfunctional." After wasting large amounts of money and feeling frustrated that the cultures in the Caribbean refuse to "do it their way," they return to the mainland angry and judgmental of the culture.

It is essential that I diffuse any notion that I am merely a cultural tourist with a self-induced epiphany. The Magnified Moments that follow are essential to the credibility of this project. As a long-term resident and participant in

the reality of everyday life in the Caribbean, I have established my most significant relationships, participated in cultural advancement as an educator, and
experienced the hardship of socioeconomic crisis. As a result, this project is
developed around two questions that have resonated with me for nearly two
decades, "Why is socioeconomic hardship a constant reality throughout the
Caribbean?" and "Is there a pathway out of the socioeconomic hardship?"

Background narrative: my first encounter (May 1994)

As the keynote speaker at a conference in Georgetown, Guyana, a prominent
Jamaican named Dr. Fedlyn Beason introduced me by stating, "*Kent may look
white, but if you cut him, he bleeds West Indian.*" How did a Caucasian male,
raised in Atlanta, Georgia, earn such a culturally distinct characterization?

After teaching advanced placement students at a private school in a suburb
of Atlanta, Georgia for five years, I was burdened by the cultural narrowness
of traditional academic pedagogy. Therefore, I made the decision to extend
the boundaries of my curriculum through an experiential learning opportunity in another culture. Based on research, Saint Paul's Episcopal School,
located in Petit Trou de Nipples, Haiti, seemed to be the ideal environment
for my sixteen students to visit and broaden their perspective of life. Three
weeks before departure (September 29, 1991), a military coup d'état removed
President Jean-Bertrand Aristide from power, which altered our plans. This
event marked my first exposure to crisis in the Caribbean. We were forced to
change our plans and select an alternate destination. We chose a school in
rural Jamaica that fit our criteria.

The Institute of the Caribbean, located in the mountains above Ocho
Rios, was a residential academic and vocational school for boys between the
ages of fifteen and nineteen years old. Due to the limited number of high
schools in Jamaica, only those who scored in the highest percentile on the
Common Entrance Exam were admitted to governmentally funded institutions. As a result, a large percentage of students in Jamaica were left without
hope of obtaining a formal education at twelve years old. The school's
mission was to provide an educational opportunity for those students who did
not meet the entrance requirements for government funded high schools.[1]
Therefore, the school relentlessly strived to fulfill the first line of its charter:
"We exist to give hope to the hopeless."

I was captivated by the school's impact on the students and the influence
on the generations that would follow. Spending two weeks at the school was
the first step into what would ultimately become my life-long passion for
education in the Caribbean. Seven months after my visit, I was asked to serve
as the Managing Director/Headmaster of the school in rural Jamaica. Without
hesitation, I agreed.

Twenty-five years after relocating, I recognize that I have established relationships that will last a lifetime and been exposed to a level of hardship that I
did not know existed. The convergence of relationship and hardship has

reconstituted my perspective of life. For every moment of crisis or conflict that I have experienced in the Caribbean, I have been privileged to participate in exponentially more wonderful moments of life and friendship. The Magnified Moments that follow represent a few of the situations that have motivated me to comprehensively analyze the relationship between creative practice and socioeconomic crisis in the Caribbean.

Magnified Moment #1: conditioned for desperation (June 1994)

After accepting the position of Managing Director/Headmaster at the Institute of the Caribbean, I sold my software training business, closed up my house in Georgia, and relocated to rural Jamaica in the fall of 1994. As my family and I deboarded the plane in Montego Bay with our ten-month-old son and seven suitcases, we headed to our new home in the lush mountains above Ocho Rios.

Our new home, which was located on the campus of the vocational school, was constructed on the property of the 300-year-old Lyford Park Great House, built by Sir Alfred DeCosta. British royalty, Jamaican Prime Ministers, Afro-Carib athletes, and renowned scholars have used the home for many of the most historic galas in the Caribbean. Characterizing the ten-bedroom house as an architectural marvel is to understate its magnificence. Eight thousand square feet of dark mahogany planks on the floor are worn with 300 years of foot traffic. The giant tapered mahogany columns that border the enormous living room support the thirty-foot-high mahogany ceilings. The royal green paint on the steep pitched metal roof is faded after many decades in the tropical climate.

Geographically positioned on the peak of a majestic countryside mountaintop, the valleys below fill with fog each morning, giving the impression that the house is floating on a cloud. As the morning fog slowly dissipates, the 360° view of the valleys, overflowing with tropical foliage illustrate the splendor of the island. "Majestic" is the adjective that visitors from all around the world have used to describe the setting, which is why the overwhelming majority expressed a desire to stay.

After the sun sets behind the lush mountains, a cool breeze threads its way throughout every room in the house, leaving behind a fragrance of tropical foliage captured from the valleys below. The crisp breeze defuses the worries of the day and eases the anxieties of tomorrow. The clarity of the heavens and the intensity of the stars illuminate the rolling hills of the mountainous terrain.

Three weeks after arriving on the island, the outgoing headmaster and I departed to the capital city of Kingston at 4:00 a.m. Since the school is located in a rural setting, a weekly trip to Kingston was required to purchase food, vocational supplies, and other needs for the school. The two and a half hour drive each way to Kingston required an early departure in order to arrive back at the school before dark. Ninety minutes after departing, we reached the Rio Cobre basin.

The Rio Cobre River, named by the Spanish to reflect the characteristics of the venomous snake, coils through the basin as a lazy "cobre" and bites with the jagged edges from its coarse rapids. The river parallels a sixteen-mile stretch of road to Kingston, of which both sides of the river are immersed with tropical fruit trees, expansive mountain ranges, and thick foliage scaling majestic stonewalls.

As we approached the eight-mile mark of the fog filled basin, the sun had yet to rise and we were making good time. Suddenly, we were forced to make an abrupt stop due to large boulders blocking the road. Perplexed, we noticed a man calmly sitting on top of the largest boulder. My colleague asked the man through his window, "What happened?" The man replied, "I blocked de road, mon, and you ain't going no further." Like a combustion engine, my colleague instantly went from complete calm to absolute anger. He screamed, "What gives you the right to block the road! Move those stones now! Are you an idiot! Move the stones! We are in a hurry!" The thought of turning back did not sit well with my colleague. Meanwhile, as the man on the rock sat calmly and listened to the spewing rage, he turned his head and whistled. Out of the rich and beautiful foliage came four other masked men all revealing pistols. They surrounded our van and demanded a "toll" to pass. The "toll" was defined as everything we had in our possession. As I sat terrified, my colleague never missed a beat in his unbridled rage. He was responding to the threat by spewing rage like a broken dam. From his perspective, the only way out of the situation was to intimidate the criminals through anger. I was certain my colleague was going to get us killed. Clearly, he had forgotten one of the tenets of the Jamaican culture, *talk and taste your tongue* (translation: think before you speak).

Unbridled rage and our hesitation to reach for our wallets prompted the gunmen to intensify their aggressiveness. A gunman from behind the van walked to my window and aimed his gun at my head. He said, "Gid me your fuck'in money now!" I responded,

> Sir, I am certain you would not be out here risking your life if you did not have a serious financial need. I am the headmaster of the school in Golden Grove and I am headed to Kingston to get supplies for students who have needs just like yours. If there are things you need, let me know and I will purchase them today. I would greatly appreciate if you would allow us to pass.

The man stepped back and quickly processed what I said. He replied, "I don't give a shit! Give me your wallet now!" As I reached for my wallet, the man sitting on the large rock, apparently the leader of the gang said, "Let dem pass!" The gunman beside my window screamed, "No!" The leader aimed his gun at the other gunman and said, "I heard de man's heart, and he is here to help us! Let dem pass!" Two men moved one of the boulders and we quickly drove through.

Exposed to a high level of chaos in the basin, my perspective of "paradise" was forever tainted; however, it prepared me for the situation that would follow later in the day. As I walked into a Burger King in Spanish Town, a small kid, maybe ten years old, pulled out a pocketknife and demanded my money. I quickly diverted his attention and took the knife out of his hand. He screamed at me, "You don't know how hungry I am!" After buying him lunch, I sat in a state of confusion. I wanted to know, "What has caused this level of desperation?"

Magnified Moment #2: left behind (1994–1997)

Since the Institute of the Caribbean Mission was well known throughout the island, admissions day was the toughest day of the year. Year after year, over 200 potential students and their guardians would travel from all over the island for a chance to be a student in the school. Many walked miles or travelled long distances in difficult forms of transportation with the hope that they would secure one of the twenty-four annual openings. The line out my office door would be hundreds of people long. Every year I would ask myself the same questions, "Why are there so many desperate people here? There are billions of tourist dollars coming into this island every year, why are kids being left behind? Shouldn't every child be guaranteed an education?"

With the high quality of instruction, four vocational trades, and employers who awarded graduates with jobs created a high demand for the twenty-four openings each year, applicants viewed the school as their last chance to rise above the hardship of their lives. Their guardians viewed the school as their only hope to rise above hardship.

After a long day of testing and interviews, I admitted the twenty-four students who scored the lowest on the placement exam based on their desire to excel academically and vocationally. Although the majority of the students who applied to the school seemed hopeless and academically deficient, they never knew that I admitted the lowest twenty-four—acceptance into the school gave the students an instant boost of confidence. At the same time, the agonizing decision to turn students away, while mothers and grandmothers pleaded with me to reconsider, motivated me to address a perplexing line of inquiry, "Why is this happening? How can a country that receives billions of tourist dollars per year not have enough schools for every student? What is the justification to leave students behind?"

Magnified Moment #3: crisis to chaos (1995)

Through fund raising efforts, hundreds of thousands of dollars had been spent making improvements to the thirteen-acre campus during my first two years at the school. The extensive improvements motivated the board of directors and me to purchase the historic property. Since the Jamaican Government had taken notice of the progress and the success of the school, they quickly negotiated a monetary value that was gracious and favorable. As soon as we signed the contract to purchase, our largest donor in Atlanta, Georgia deposited $109,000 into the school's Jamaican bank account for the down payment. While I was waiting for the attorneys to schedule the closing, I was elated to find out that the money was earning 26% interest in the local bank. Although everything was falling into place to ensure the school's long-term stability, the high interest rate seemed too good to be true.

Four months after the money was deposited, the morning headline in the local newspaper read, "Banking Regulators have closed the third largest bank in Jamaica." The bank that closed was the Century National Bank, who had possession of our funds to purchase the property, general operating accounts (which included payroll), and personal accounts. Every penny that belonged to the school and I was sealed away in a bank that regulators stated would not reopen—a single decision made by a panel of five people placed the school in the direst of straights. My first question was, "How could this happen?" After the shock softened and the reality of the crisis set in, I angrily asked, "How am I going to feed sixty people three meals per day, make payroll for twenty employees, and pay exorbitantly high utilities with no money?" For weeks, everyone associated with the school asked the same question again and again, "Why do these situations keep happening in our country?"

Twenty-six months later, 80% of the money was returned through a government settlement. The remaining 20% and the interest were never recovered. Once again, I was overwhelmed at how quickly crisis could become a state of chaos. As with many crises in the region, the majority of the bank's depositors were hard-working people struggling to survive. A single decision by a government agency to close one bank created widespread hardship throughout the island, which further deepened the level of poverty and perpetuated hardship. The hardship that the Afro-Carib culture endures naturally generates an unanswered question: "Why are we suffering through financial crisis four decades after independence?"

Magnified Moment #4: inconceivable measures (1995)

From my perspective, to effectively lead the Institute of the Caribbean required an understanding of daily life in Jamaica. Seeking to develop a rapport with the parents or guardians of each student in the school, I often accepted invitations to visit the homes of students for tea or a meal. All of those moments shaped my understanding and compassion for the reality of life in the Caribbean.

After accepting an invitation, I arrived at Eric Traille's farm in York Castle captivated by the area's piercing beauty. The isolated 350-year-old farming village sits abreast one of the most beautiful settings in the world. Even though it is difficult to reach the village, the 4,000-foot elevation, cool temperatures, and lush tropical environment made York Castle the ideal place for the first high school in Jamaica. Although the historic boarding school closed its doors in 1901, every visitor that journeys into the humble village must pass by the ruins of the school's past grandeur and excellence. Surely the vivid realization drives every visitor to ask, "What happened? How could this vital agricultural region of the island be so suppressed?"

Eric was a Jamaican who had lived all fifty-four years of his life in York Castle. I had the privilege of getting to know Eric in my office when he came to inquire about the academic progress of his son. Recognizing that he did not have an automobile, which meant a forty-five-minute walk to a thoroughfare to "hitch a ride," then travel another forty-five minutes in an overcrowded van to the school, I was honored to give him my undivided attention and accept an invitation to his home.

Prior to walking to his mountainside farm from his house, we sat on his front porch drinking freshly squeezed fruit punch in order to sufficiently hydrate for the Jamaican heat. Our conversation revealed that Eric was a simple man who possessed a profound understanding of life. He and his wife had eight children; one of his children was handicapped and required full-time assistance. Eric told me,

> The medication to ease my son's chorea is less than a dollar per pill in other parts of the world, but it's not available in Jamaica and I can't afford to have it shipped here. As a result, my son constantly injures himself on the bed, against walls, and on the floor due to uncontrollable movements. Most of the world believes that life is easy in Jamaica, but for some reason life is not easy in Jamaica, Kent.

Once again, I asked myself, "Why is this happening?"

We finished our fruit punch, gathered the necessary tools, and began the mile-long walk to reach his farm. Walking along the narrow, mountainside path I thought about the paradox of Eric's life: on the one hand he lives in a farming village that most would characterize as impoverished; on the other hand his family and disposition define him as a man who was rich in contentment and confidence. Once we arrived, I was awestruck by the sacrifice this man had made for over thirty years.

Cultivating a farm that is only accessible by foot means that tools, water, pesticides, and the harvest have to be carried in and out by hand. Maybe it was the reason why Eric had hands of might and was absurdly strong at fifty-four years old. However, I was humbled most by his resolve to ensure stability for his family and community. Every function of this man's life seemed to be a strategic plan to give life to others. Even though he and his entire village were subjected to the crisis of a debilitating economy, to live life another way was incomprehensible to this man. As a result, his station in life seemed to have no influence over his happiness or satisfaction.

He appeared unshakable, no matter what was gathering at his flank or looming on the horizon.

As we worked on the hillside farm, Eric began to pull the large yams from the ground, cut a sizable piece with his machete, and bury the remaining piece attached to the vine back in the ground. As I packed the harvest into large burlap bags, Eric systematically cut and harvested cho-cho, pumpkin, cassava, and callalou. When he was done, I counted six large heavy bags full of "the fruits of his labor." We sat for a few minutes, hydrated ourselves, threw a bag over our shoulder, and began the trip back to the village. As I walked down the rugged path ahead of Eric, I tried my best not to show how difficult it was to carry the weighty bag over my shoulder. When I turned to make sure Eric was ok, my ego was deflated. I was thirty-two years old; Eric was fifty-four. I worked out daily and considered myself to be in very good physical condition. Eric not only had a bag over each shoulder, but was also carrying tools under each of his arms! I had convinced myself that I was "carrying my weight, showing my worth." After making the one-mile trip back to his house, Eric sat the bags down and said, "I will be back in a few minutes." He was headed back to get the other three bags. Refusing to show fatigue, I went with him.

After a day of farming, we took refuge from the sun on his porch where we drank a cup of Red Rose tea and ate freshly made Johnny Cakes. Before I made the trip back to the school Eric asked me to take a walk through the village. As we were walking we purchased a grapefruit drink called Ting in a small shop, then sat on the steps of the shop mesmerized by the view. The majestic mountain ranges, small villages that weaved through the valleys, remarkable birds floating in the sky, and the abounding tropical foliage made the moment seem surreal. As Eric pointed out important geographical locations below, I distinctly recall telling myself, "Do not forget this moment. Store it in a permanent place of memory." Suddenly, Eric shifted his dialogue from the other villages and focused on York Castle. He humbly said to me,

> Our town is in trouble. We are a community completely dependent upon farming in an economy that is out of control. We have a meeting tonight about the situation. Would you please come and talk about ideas that may help us grow?

What I encountered that night reconstituted my perspective of crisis.

Later that evening at the meeting each man respectfully stood and expressed his concern about the future of their village. At that moment, I realized that as an American I took for granted the great generosity of the nation in which I was born. There would be no bailout funds for this community, Neil Young would not be organizing a Farm Aid, and no assistance for the handicapped or the poor would be coming through any social service. Every family was in full survival mode and their desperation was in full view. The families had nowhere to turn but to themselves. Unfortunately, even their most prized possessions, their farms, were a source of immense discouragement. I kept asking myself the same question that each of these men must have asked thousands of times, "What happened? I'm sitting in a land of abundant resources, beauty beyond description, yet hopelessness abounds. How did this happen?"

Since the 1990s the Jamaican economy has continued to spiral out of control—the exchange rate between the United States currency and Jamaican dollar has changed considerably: 7 to 1 in 1990, 35 to 1 in 1995, 43 to 1 in 2000, and 85 to 1 in 2010 (Bank of Jamaica, 2016).[2] Meanwhile, island-grown food prices have remained relatively static which means that the families in the farming community of York Castle could no longer depend on earning their livelihood from the soil—agriculture has been the source of sustainable support for many generations. In all of my life I have never witnessed hopelessness like I encountered that night. I did not say a word at the meeting and spent the time grieving over the errant perception of "paradise."

As I drove home from York Castle, I continued to be troubled by the same question: "Why is this rich culture struggling to survive?" After watching Eric function in an environment saturated in crisis, I learned a valuable lesson from a farmer in rural Jamaica. Eric recognized that neither foliage nor geography defines a vibrant life, rather the life we have is to be given to those around us. At that moment I began to understand that I could take a position of passivity and ignore the reality of crisis, or I could allow my ambitions to be focused on understanding the crisis in the Caribbean and search for a path of sustainable growth.

Magnified Moment #5: following the master (1995)

As I slept comfortably in the cool Jamaican mountain air I was suddenly awakened by a piercing reality at 2:38 a.m.—the sound of a car accident on the road behind the school. From my window I could see strewn wreckage and hear faint moans for help. The unmistakable sound immediately prompted me to hastily make the five-minute walk to the bridge.

Reaching the main road, a friend informed me that a car was traveling too fast around the sharp turn and drifted from the road in front of the bridge. The car plummeted nose first, sixty feet onto an old concrete mining road below. Arriving less than five minutes after the crash I was stunned by what I witnessed. People were engulfing the car, frantically removing any items of value—like ants attacking an open sugar bowl. The back wheels were being unbolted, the passenger seat was being unfastened, the stereo removed, and the contents of the trunk were being looted. Tragically, this activity was happening while the driver lay dead against the steering wheel. I was horrified at the savage behavior and disappointed that my image of the culture was forever altered.

Disgusted, I left the dreadful tragedy for the peace of my bed. Walking through "the bush" to reach the road, I noticed a small fire burning in front of a tin shack on the hillside. Sitting beside the fire was a Rastafarian with long flowing dreadlocks smoking his spiritual herb. The simplicity of his shack reflected his faithfulness to his Rastafarian beliefs. He was choosing to live a minimalist life as a sojourner in this materialistically driven world. The Rastaman also watched the horrific events unfold—I wondered what he was thinking? As I stared up the hill, the Rastaman and I made eye contact, nodded our heads in respect, and moved on from the moment.

As I slowly walked back to the school reflecting on what I had witnessed under the bridge, questions began to abound—What if that man in the car had a family or kids, how were they going to feel when they realized that their father's possessions were pillaged as he laid dying against the steering wheel? I knew nothing about that man who died, but he could have been hurrying home to see his family. He might have been tired from working two jobs and fell asleep at the wheel. Yet, these people were at the scene of the tragedy within minutes, as if they were prepared to pounce the moment they heard tragedy or witnessed vulnerability. How does someone become what I just witnessed? Is it possible that these people were emulating the observations of the past?

Lying in bed, I can hear the laughter of celebration from those acting as if they have won a battle. For some twisted reason they believed they had conquered the moment and improved their lives. My portrait of peace was forever stained by the intensity of chaos.

Magnified Moment #6: soil, seeds, and roots (1995)

One year after relocating from the deep south of the United States to the rural mountains of Jamaica, I made my first significant financial decision as the Managing Director of the Institute of the Caribbean. Since the entire student body and faculty lived on campus, the school served three meals per day, seven days per week. Managing the historic thirteen-acre campus with an academic school and four vocational tracks—welding, woodworking, horticulture, and auto mechanics—in a country where the cost of living was exorbitant required me to be creative in the way I expended resources. Since food was the largest annual budgetary line item, I made a decision to grow our food instead of purchasing it at the high priced markets.

Through a meticulous three-month process, we constructed a retaining wall, prepared the soil, and planted the seeds on a beautiful rolling knoll adjacent to the Great House. As plant life began to peak through the dark soil, I zealously strategized a new budget. Adding a new vocational building, completing the dining hall, paving the treacherous driveway, repairing the greenhouse, remodeling the kitchen and completing the staff dormitory were all long overdue projects and could be accomplished with the additional funds in the budget.

Due to rich volcanic soil and a perfect growing climate, within a month the garden was maturing and showing signs of "bearing fruit." Within two months the lettuce, cabbage, sweet potatoes, yams, cho-cho, corn, beans, okra, peppers, onions, and tomatoes were within weeks of their first harvest. Since the garden was right below my bedroom windows, each morning I would gaze out the window and find a fresh new dose of satisfaction. My first significant financial decision as the head of the school was appearing to be a huge success.

Several mornings later, I looked out the window for a glimpse of the garden to find horror. Approximately one-third of the plants—hundreds—had vanished. I ran out to the knoll and found evidence of animals in the garden. I immediately walked the periphery of the thirteen acres searching for a hole in the fence or animals that might have pushed their way through. Nothing, not one downed fence pole or breech in the fence was found.

Determined to find out why the garden was disappearing in huge increments, the next morning I positioned myself at 5:00 a.m. in the middle of the garden thinking about shattered dreams and unmet expectations. Out in the distance, movement by the road caught my eye. Through the fog I could faintly see the Rastaman who lived on top of the adjacent mountain walking his forty plus goats along the road. I could hear him jubilantly singing a legendary reggae tune about redemption. Walking with a casual pace, his goats were obediently following him on their morning stroll.

Suddenly, the Rastaman stopped, opened the gate into our pasture, and guided his goats straight to our garden. Furious, I responded by throwing stones at the goats and screaming at the Rastaman. The goats scattered and the Rastaman was enraged that I had struck a member of his herd with a stone. He screamed at me from one knoll and I screamed back from the other. Like all Third World herders, the Rastaman was carrying a machete. Suddenly, he began to run down the knoll directly at me with his machete elevated in strike position. Fully engaged in fury I responded by running straight toward him. As we met in the valley between the two knolls, one of the students who overheard the conflict ran to help me. Nose to nose yelling at each other, the Rastaman kept the machete in strike position while he screamed at me in his deep patois dialect. Since I had no idea what he was saying, I turned to the student and asked for interpretation. The student said, "Mr. Kent, he is cursing every member of your family—I think you should RUN!" The student ran away and left me standing with the vexed man who appeared ready to strike me down. Recognizing that my response to this conflict was errant and ineffective, which negated any reasonable conclusion, I turned and walked back to the house. Later that afternoon I sealed off the gate.

The next morning about the same time, I heard someone screaming out on the road. To my astonishment, it was the Rastafarian standing at the sealed gate. He was beyond angry that the gate was sealed and his goats were not being fed. I went back into the house, prepared a cup of tea, and listened to the Rastaman scream insults for another two hours.

Every morning for the next year, the Rastaman stood on the road in front of the school and yelled, "Slave master! Boys, rise up against the White slave driver! Strike the slave master down!" The Rastaman's hostility was directed at my ethnicity; a point of reference that set me apart from the rest of the school's population; all the students, staff, and faculty were Jamaican. The "Great House" that the faculty, students, and my family lived in was constructed in colonial times for colonial purposes. The symbolism of my skin color, my refusal to allow his goats to feed on land he believed belonged to his people, and the presence of the colonial house on the hill seemed to stir generational fury in the Rastaman.

However, due to my failure to engage him through respect and dialogue when his goats were in our garden, I forfeited the opportunity for him to know my true intentions in Jamaica. Although I was the only white man at the school, I was hired by, and accountable to, a Jamaican Board of Directors. The Board was a group of successful Jamaican business owners, educators, clergy and politicians. If there were any impropriety in my intentions or leadership, they would have been quick to correct or remove me from the position.

Inflaming the situation further, the Rastaman frequently waited at the end of our driveway and told students as they walked to town for snacks, "You are the slaves to that white man! The man is a slave master!" He told them, "Flee from oppression or rise up against the slave driver!" He stood on the road during academic periods and yelled, "Slave driver must die!"

When the Rastaman recognized that his methods were not working he took his attack to another level. The Rastaman hid behind an almond tree at the top of our driveway and waited for me to pass. As I stopped our van to open the gates into the school, the Rastaman jumped out with his machete and acted as if he was going to kill me. I jumped into the van and quickly drove up to the house. I responded by grabbing a machete from the basement and began running back down the driveway like two medieval enemies ready to settle a score with blood. The Rastaman had not moved from his original position and appeared ready to engage me in a physical conflict. A year of name-calling had reached its limit with me. Since I knew my intentions in Jamaica were pure, I too was ready for a physical confrontation.

As I approached the Rastaman, the students ran out of their classrooms and began to shout, "Go, Mr. Kent! Beat him bloody, mon!" Through all the screaming emotion I heard a familiar voice scream, "Daddy! What are you doing Daddy?" Over sixty voices were supporting my anger inspired response; but my son's voice seemed to rise above the chaos. The combination of the students on one side and the Rastaman on the other fueled my anger, but my son's voice instantly made me pause to assess the situation. I stopped about twenty steps from the Rastaman. As a role model to young men who were desperate for a responsible male figurehead in their lives, I stood still and reconsidered my next step—"Am I going to be part of the solution to hardship or an instigator of chaos?"

I turned around to walk back to the house. Shortly after I turned, Rastaman threw a coconut and hit me in the back. I paused, processed, and kept walking. When I reached the top of the driveway one of the staff members said, "Yu made a good decision to turn back. Never forget, Yu lie wit dawg, yu rise wit fleas."

Several days later, as the students, faculty, and staff ate dinner in the outdoor dining hall, the Rastaman began to yell at me from atop his mountain, "Rise up me boi's, rise up! You are the white man's slaves!" As he was yelling a car pulled into the school's driveway and out stepped a friendly face with a huge smile, R. E. Lee. Mr. Lee was a Board member and Jamaican businessman who I had visited in his home on many occasions.

After preparing him a plate of food we sat down to visit. Just a few bites into his meal he asked, "Who is yelling at you, mon?" The other faculty members pointed to the Rastaman and began to tell Mr. Lee what he had been doing to me for over a year. Mr. Lee got up from the table with his meal half eaten and left in his car. We all watched him drive on the road around the school and stop at the bottom of the mountain where the Rastaman lived. He got out of his car and walked to the top of the steep hill. We could faintly see and hear them arguing, until they abruptly sat down. They sat on large stones and talked for about fifteen minutes. When they stood again, they descended down the mountain and entered Mr. Lee's car together.

Watching them drive on the road in front of the school, there was a unanimous feeling in the dining hall that Mr. Lee was driving the Rastaman to another parish to make him "disappear." A student stood on a chair and yelled, "Rasta! Yu finally gett'in what yu deserve!" To everyone's astonishment, when they reached the driveway with the Rastaman in the passenger seat, they turned in and passed through the gates to the school. Due to the events of the last year I thought it best that I walk out and meet them when they reached the top of the driveway.

With more than sixty people in the outdoor dining hall watching twenty feet away, Mr. Lee and the Rastaman stepped out of the car. Mr. Lee said,

> Kent, this is Egbert. Egbert grew up in a very rural part of the island called Cockpit. Egbert wants you to know he is a businessman who sells coal for open air cooking pits, just like the one you built for the school. I told him you might be interested in becoming a customer. What do you think?

I was completely speechless. My mind was stumbling to process what was transpiring in front of the entire student body. The only word that could find a way out of my mouth was, "Ok".

Egbert and Mr. Lee got back into the car and drove back to the Egbert's mountain. Mr. Lee came back, sat down at the table where his food was half eaten, finished his dinner, tutored a few students, and drove home.

The next afternoon, I witnessed human transformation like never before. Walking down our 700-foot driveway, dressed in clean clothes and no machete, was Egbert with a large burlap bag over his shoulder. He came to bring coal for the large outdoor grill. When he reached the top of the driveway I extended my hand and said, "How are you today, Egbert?" He shook my hand in return and said, "I am blessed, mon. I came to give you some extra coal I had." I thanked him and asked him if he would join us for dinner? As we ate together all eyes were intently focused on us.

When Egbert finished eating, the student body, unprompted, came one by one and greeted him. I then walked with Egbert to the end of driveway with faculty and students looking on from the windows of the school. I took advantage of the peaceful reconciliation and said to Egbert, "When I threw stones at your goats I was wrong. When I argued with you in the pasture I was wrong. I'm asking you to forgive my behavior." Egbert put out his hand and said, "Respect, mon." We shook hands and went our way.

I retreated to my room in awe, noting that a simple act of respect would have diffused the chaos from the beginning; however, my response opened the door for a year-long tirade. From that day forward all the cooking coal at the school was purchased from Egbert. Egbert ate one meal per day with us at the school, he volunteered in the garden, and because of the geographical vantage point of his home he caught several people "teifing" (stealing) things from the school.

Reflecting back on the conflict many months later, I remained perplexed at why it took Egbert so long to let go of the matter? Could it be that the generations of oppression have legitimately uprooted trust for outside cultures? At some point, I understood that my presence as a white man represented the soil of the past, which meant that I had to consistently plant seeds of respectful communication at all times. Finally, as I began to slowly understand the culture and its tragic identity of oppression, I contemplated the reality of everyday life for the people in the Caribbean. Since the region is considered a mecca of tourism, how many times per day are the individuals in the Caribbean demeaned by haughty visitors on their respective islands? Due to the horrid colonial roots of the past, should anyone blame the cultures of the Caribbean for being confrontational when disrespected? Since the colonial past is a reality and the economies of the Caribbean are dependent upon the presence of tourists, it seems inevitable that communication will continue to be a point of conflict—adding another layer to the most commonly asked question in the Caribbean, "Why is all this happening to us?"

Magnified Moment #7: shallow intentions (1996)

When I was invited to observe a friend's sugar cane farm in 1996, we navigated the rugged terrain of the Cockpit country into a valley called Vale of Lluidas. The Worthy Park Estate is a 3,600-hectare (8,892 acres) farm that was established in 1660. After spending several days at the farm observing the processes of harvesting sugar cane, conversion to molasses, and manufacturing of rum, I ventured into an Anglican church located on the farm. The small stone church was built the same year the farm was established (1660). Located on a shelf in the front corner of the church was a large book (approximately ten inches thick, one foot wide and two feet tall) with the following inscription on the front, "Records of Birth – Worthy Park, Jamaica".

Examining the pages, I counted sixty hand-written entries per page. One of the headings asked, "Are the parents married?" Although I was not certain, I assumed the reasoning behind the question was moral since the log was kept in a church. With sixty entries on both sides of the page, I had to turn back forty-four pages to find a "Y" reply. The reply was dated, "24-October-69." Another heading asked, "Number of siblings?' The reference was the number of siblings for the newborn child. On each of the forty-four pages I turned back, no page had less than four entries with double-digit answers for the sibling question.

My final observation was the small schoolhouse adjacent to the church. The owner of the farm informed me that the school, which has been closed for fifteen years, covered grades one through three. In the colonial period, after the few "privileged" slaves learned to read and write, their education was complete and they were placed into the production process at the farm.

The experience at the farm caused me to ask the following question;

> It has been thirty-four years since this country signed its declaration of independence; why is this rich culture with bountiful resources still struggling to survive? Could it be that the culture was strategically and tragically shaped to rely solely on the might of muscle?

Magnified Moment #8: creative continuum of influence—Jamaica (2003)

When the Lydford Park Great House was constructed nearly 350 years ago in the rural mountains above Ocho Rios, Jamaica, a natural crossroads developed just outside the boundaries of the property.[3] The Golden Grove crossroads remains an active thoroughfare for travelers navigating the island's winding, mountainous terrain. The west road of the crossroads navigates through the tropical foliage to St. Ann's Bay, the location that many historians believe Columbus first encountered Jamaica. The north road passes through an adjacent mountain range, spills out onto a diverted riverbed called Fern Gully, and ends in the town of Ocho Rios. The east road is the most traveled and commonly called the "road to town," which leads to Kingston, the capital of Jamaica. The south road is a scenic mountain route through the majestic mountains of inner Jamaica. Nine miles south of the crossroads is a farming village called Nine Mile, the birthplace of Robert (Bob) Nesta Marley.

Leading a school nine miles from Bob Marley's birthplace and mausoleum meant many of my guests wanted to pay homage to Marley by visiting the inspirational site of much of his music. As a result, I travelled to Nine Mile often, formed significant relationships in the area, and visited the Marley site many times. When a Rastafarian friend from Tortola, British Virgin Islands expressed a desire to "make a pilgrimage to the holy site," he requested that I accompany him to Nine Mile. After escorting him to Nine Mile I arranged for us to receive a private tour of the Marley estate.

When we entered the Ethiopian inspired chapel on the peak of the site our attention quickly turned to a table in the foyer. The table was lined with wood containers overflowing with ganja from the island and beyond.[4] Although I do not smoke ganja or share Marley's philosophical position, the chapel, which houses Marley's mausoleum, is a work of art to behold. The exterior walls are lined with opulent stained glass windows. The rows of handcrafted pews made from local woods are for meditation. The gold-laced altar around Marley's tomb is lined with peace offerings representing cultures from every continent on earth. The Marley Chapel is a place where Rastafarian sojourners from all over the world gather, meditate, and smoke the "herb of enlightenment."

When my friend was settled and fulfilling his spiritual experience, I left the chapel in a reflective awe—how could someone from such a poor rural agricultural mountain village in Jamaica, born during a colonial occupation, inspire millions around the world through his music? The enormous global influence of Marley's creativity juxtaposed to his cultural surroundings was beyond my grasp.

As I sat on the rock where Marley wrote *No Woman No Cry*, I began to identify sources of inspiration for Marley—the hardship of the rural setting, a simple way of life, the passionate disposition of the Jamaican culture, and the flowing hillsides covered with yam, coco, banana, and cannabis plants. Although Marley is legitimately accredited as being a musical genius, his creative expression seemed to be a continuum of his culture. The accentuated themes of Marley's music suggest that he valued his culture as a treasured asset. However, as I witnessed sojourners from around the world unload from the tour buses, it was obvious that Marley's creative achievement reached beyond the borders of Jamaica.

Marley's creative expression constructed a global movement. He motivated generations of people to engage in collective actions of expression, narrative, and investment. He created a genre of music that inspired musicians from many diverse cultures to emulate as a creative expression. His music exposed tens of millions to his island culture, which created a global narrative regarding the hardship of the Caribbean peoples. Due to the heightened awareness of his culture, millions of people visit Jamaica annually, thus corporations have invested vast resources to build hotels, resorts, and venues of entertainment. Inspired by the reality of life in his small mountain village, Marley's creative expression had a global socioeconomic affect that elevated the lives of many.

As I sat on the rock and tried to put the scope and scale of Marley's influence in perspective, I questioned why Marley's continuum of creativity seemed to be an isolated phenomenon in the Caribbean? Could Marley's continuum of culturally influenced creativity be a model for other elements within the culture? If so, could the continuum be a legitimate source to ease the longstanding socioeconomic hardship for the cultures of the Caribbean?

Magnified Moment #9: opportunity deprivation (2010)

After leaving Jamaica in 1997, my love for the Caribbean cultures extended to the Lesser Antilles. I first settled on Tortola in the British Virgin Islands, then onto Saint John in the United States Virgin Islands. I held educational-based positions on both islands, Gifft Hill School and the University of the Virgin Islands. My cumulative life experiences in the Caribbean as a parent, educator, and leader enabled me to recognize an area of need within the culture—organized extracurricular opportunities for children on small islands were sparse. As a result of a lack of opportunities, families with financial means or relatives living in the United States, Canada, or Europe frequently sent their children abroad in order to participate in extracurricular activities.

One sunny afternoon I was on the Julius S. Sprauve school field in Cruz Bay, St. John throwing a football with my ten-year-old son. Fifteen minutes later, more than twenty kids were playing football with us on the field. I played quarterback for both teams for an hour, then retreated to the stands to catch my breath. As I sat on the bleachers watching the kids play on a field with no grass, no chalked lines, strewn garbage, a broken scoreboard, and a falling fence, I understood the frustration expressed by the community.

Three feet from where I sat, there was a rat eating a half-eaten hamburger bun. Behind me, the concession stand was covered in cockroaches and the garbage bins reeked of rotten food. Everywhere I looked I smelled death; yet the field was full of kids who longed for life. At that moment I was once again faced with a repetitive quandary, I could passively ignore the reality and retreat into my "island life," or I could become part of the solution.

I chose the latter and partnered with Mr. Brummell Germain to organize a football league for kids. On the day of registration, I was privileged to observe authentic transformation—frowns to smiles, disappointment to excitement, and idleness to activity. Men who were habitually leaving work for their televisions volunteered to coach teams. Parents lined up along the roadside fence eager to give me their registration forms. Ecstatic kids were jostling for position and humorously overstating their abilities. The first moment of transformation was a "sweet ting, me boi."

The days ahead were exciting; I could not escape parents and kids calling out to me as I walked along the streets. Grateful people stopped me daily on the road to say, "Thank You" and "How can I help?" My cell phone was inundated with calls from eager players regarding schedules and team rosters.

Several minutes prior to the first game, I noticed that the motions and fragrances of life consumed the moment. The fragrance of fresh cooked food flowing from the concession stand filled Cruz Bay. The smell of crisp new uniforms empowered the eager players. The aroma of fresh chalk on the field meant one thing—game day. The kids were nervously sweating, the coaches were uptight about their game plans, and the referees were eager to get started. Sixty kids, droves of parents, coaches, referees, and spectators were collectively experiencing life in downtown Cruz Bay.

As the teams were taking the field I wondered if a player or two would convert their love for the game into a college scholarship one day. Or maybe a relationship being formed in a huddle would turn into a life-long friendship. Maybe the multi-cultured life lessons of team play would catapult a young man into success later in his life. Maybe the accountability demanded by a team sport would teach a young man to make the right decisions in the years ahead. On and around the football field, life flowed in all directions and had no boundaries.

As the first games concluded, fragrances of new life thrived. The smell of sweat represented hard work. The scents of dirt and blood meant sacrifice. As I was about to leave the field for dinner, I noticed the stench of my hands from patting sweating backs, shaking sweating hands, and giving high fives. As I went to wash my hands I realized the smell emanating from my hands was a sweet aroma to my emotions. A repulsive scent to others symbolized the first step of community transformation and satisfaction to me. As I reached for the soap to wash my hands, I placed the soap back on the sink and chose to eat with hands that represented life. I walked across the street from the field, picked bananas, and sat down in the bleachers overlooking the field. I ate the fresh fruit while gratefully recognizing that I was a participant in a life-giving moment—an opportunity that was transformed into a reality.

Four years later, the league grew to over 200 kids and became a primary social outlet on the island. Every Friday night in Cruz Bay, five months out of every year, the league brought together all cultures on the island. Many players went on to play high school football on St. Thomas, some earned scholarships to college, and others learned the value of intercultural team play. On Father's Day in 2011, I was honored to receive thirty-nine text messages from kids in the league telling me how much they appreciated my sacrifice and contribution to their lives.

Finally, the poor condition of the field was a source of community disappointment for over thirty years. The success of the league motivated one of its players to give new life to the dead, stony field. Prior to the fifth season, one of the players chose the field for his science project in school. Iowa State University took notice and with the sacrifice of many in the St John community, the field was graded and reseeded with drought resistant grass. A thirty-year-old eye sore in the heart of the community was restored to give life to generations of kids.

When I reflect back on the years that I was privileged to provide an opportunity for the children of St John, I could not help but wonder why the scarcity of opportunities for the children of the islands continues to be scarce? Why are kids de-prioritized in government budgets and structures? Why is this happening in "paradise?"

Magnified Moment #1:
Conditioned for Desperation
Jamaica (1994)

How did the moment modify my personal perspective of paradise?
a. "Paradise" seems to be an illusion.
b. Desperateness has no boundaries.

Magnified Moment #2:
Left Behind
Jamaica (1994)

How did the moment modify my personal perspective of paradise?
a. Hopelessness seems to be a prevailing reality in the Caribbean.
b. Someone has to be brave enough to construct a better reality.

Magnified Moment #3:
Crisis to Chaos
Jamaica (1995)

How did the moment modify my personal perspective of paradise?
a. Do not assume anything is secure in the Caribbean.
b. Conscious resilience is a necessity of survival in the Caribbean.

Magnified Moment #4:
Inconceivable Measures
Jamaica (1995)

How did the moment modify my personal perspective of paradise?
a. Life is not easy in the Caribbean.
b. Hospitality and hopelessness seem to be a way of life.

Magnified Moment #5:
Following the Master
Jamaica (1995)

How did the moment modify my personal perspective of paradise?
a. Generational suffering has created unimaginable patterns of behavior.
b. Patterns of behavior seem to be the result of a long-established
environment of violence.

Figure 2.1 Summary of Magnified Moments.

Magnified Moment #6:
Soil, Seeds, and Roots
Jamaica (1995)

How did the moment modify my personal perspective of paradise?
a. My presence as a white man symbolized a horrid past, which legitimately mandated respectful communication, no matter the circumstances of the moment.
b. Generations of oppression have legitimately eroded trust for outside cultures.
c. One brave person can stop the crisis.

Magnified Moment #7:
Shallow Intentions
Jamaica (1996)

How did the moment modify my personal perspective of paradise?
a. The reality of imperialistic oppression remains relevant to the current environment.
b. Long term oppression was strategic.

Magnified Moment #8:
Creative Continuum of Influence
Jamaica (2003)

How did the moment modify my personal perspective of paradise?
a. Creative expressions derived from cultural experience have the potential to affect the socioeconomic reality for many generations.

Magnified Moment #9:
Opportunity Deprivations
St. John, U.S. Virgin Islands (2010)

How did the moment modify my personal perspective of paradise?
a. There is a passionate grassroots desire for change in the Caribbean; however, many have abandoned hope for change and migrated for opportunities for personal growth.
b. Transformation is within the realm of possibility.

Figure 2.1 Continued

Having the privilege to live amongst and be accepted in the Afro-Carib culture for nearly two decades is one of the great honors of my life. Sacrificing for the culture continues to be my passionate mission. Although I have achieved several academic accolades in the Caribbean, my greatest academic accomplishment would be to develop a viable sustainable response to the socioeconomic hardship for the people in the region. Thus, my positionality remains a catalyst in exposing the components of sustainable growth and the sources of, "Why is this happening in the Caribbean?"

Notes

1 After my departure from Jamaica, the school progressed through a series of headmasters. The headmaster installed in 2002 systematically pilfered the assets of the school to support his personal lifestyle. When confronted, he committed suicide and forced the school to close.
2 This trend is owed to the IMF's structural adjustment program, to make imports expensive and exports cheaper. This, the IMF insists even today, will make the poor people in the Caribbean richer. This is a deliberate Word Bank, IMF and US policy toward the Caribbean (Fitzroy Beckford, PhD).
3 The Lydford Park Great House was home to the Institute of Caribbean Mission— the school in which I was the Headmaster/Managing Director.
4 Ganja: marijuana. Reference Glossary B.

References

Bank of Jamaica (2016). Historical Rates: Jamaica dollar vs. United States dollar: December 31, 1971 to January 31, 2016. Retrieved from www.boj.org.jm/foreign_exchange/fx_historical_rates.php

Creswell, J. (1998). *Qualitative inquiry and research design: Choosing among five traditions.* London: Sage.

Worthy Park Estate. (n.d.). Retrieved from http://worthyparkestate.biz/index.php

3 "Paradise" lost in crisis—a historical progression of the Caribbean

Extraordinary innovation, creative methods, and complex technology continue to fuel the growth trajectories of first world nations, while a relevant question remains unanswered in the Caribbean, "Have forty million people been left behind in regard to global development?" Long-term hardship, global misunderstanding, and lingering points of crisis suggest that the region has been left behind and remains underdeveloped. Ironically, the global community overwhelmingly views the region as their playground in "paradise," yet the reality of life for the Africans in the Caribbean is one steeped in long-term socioeconomic crisis.[1]

When the Afro-Carib Nobel Laureate, Derek Walcott (1984), characterized the reality of "paradise," he defined the Caribbean, specifically the United States Virgin Islands, as possessing two distinctly different perspectives: "the beaches and harbors are for white Americans seeking the sun, but black Afro-Caribs see it as a stepping stone, a place to wait for a few years before moving northward" (p. 68). Walcott's position affirms a perplexing reality in the Caribbean: more residents migrate from the Caribbean than any other region in the world, yet thirty million tourists visited the region in 2014 (Caribbean Tourism Quality Index, 2015). While tourists flock to the beaches and bars in "paradise," the Afro-Caribs exit their beloved island nations seeking relief from crisis and opportunities for personal growth.

After observing the culture suffer through escalating hardship for most of my adult life, I still hear the same repetitive question in reference to the reality of life in the Caribbean, "Why is all this hardship happening to us?" A historical progression of the region provides texture and understanding to the hardship that affects nearly 40 million residents. Understanding the 500 year history of the Caribbean is to understand that "paradise" for the Africans in the Caribbean has been perpetually defined as survival, resistance, violence, oppression, crisis, chaos, and dependency—prevailing themes that I observed as a resident. Although the five distinct historical periods of the Caribbean clarify *why* the Africans in the Caribbean continue to suffer through socioeconomic crisis, they also illuminate a solution. Therefore, the most important question regarding the African culture in the Caribbean is, "Who will have the courage to end the crisis?"

This brief picture of the history of the Caribbean is a reflection of the events that transpired on every colonized island in the region—the horrific events on one island were reflected on all the colonized islands. Further, the residual effects of the crisis and chaos generated by the imperial oppressors remains a consistent impediment to growth and independence throughout the Caribbean (Girvan, 2012). In the context of this project, the observed themes from my positionality will be juxtaposed to the themes from the historical progression to illuminate any points of commonality.

Encounter Era (1492–1501): birth of crisis and chaos in the Caribbean

> The ancient civilisations in the Caribbean, and others, helped shape the way society was organised, how work, money and the economy were planned, and how human culture was created and developed.
>
> (Beckles & Shepherd, 2004, p. 1)

Thinking he was in East Asia, Columbus and his three ships anchored off an island called Guanahani in the Bahamas on October 12, 1492 (Monzote, 2011). Expecting to find vast amounts of commodities and extreme wealth, he discovered an undisturbed, indigenous culture. Recognizing that he was the first European to encounter the indigenous culture in this new part of the world, he wrote about the monumental moment in his journal. In a section addressed to King Ferdinand and Queen Isabella, Columbus described the Taíno Indians as follows:

> They traded with us and gave us everything they had, with good will … they took great delight in pleasing us. They are very gentle and without knowledge of what is evil; nor do they murder or steal.… Your highness may believe that in all the world there can be no better people.… They love their neighbours as themselves, and they have the sweetest talk in the world, and are gentle and always laughing.
>
> (Sale, 1991, p. 100)

Although Columbus' initial response seemed ideal, it is important to note that the encounter set in motion conditions that would result in 500 years of increasing crisis and chaos throughout the Caribbean.

Writing about the same encounter, Columbus noted that the Taínos "lacked tools made with iron, not so much because he sought to trade, but rather because it implied that they had no weapons to fear or defend themselves—no guns, no swords, no crossbows" (Higman, 2011, p. 59). Columbus further stated, "I could conquer the whole of them with fifty men and govern them as I please" (Columbus & Tosconelli, 2010, p. 41). Higman (2011), a historian who has comprehensively analyzed the Caribbean, offers an interpretation of Columbus's remarks: "He immediately saw them as potentially well fitted for labour" (p. 60). The horrific events that define Caribbean Colonialism seemed to have been birthed the moment that Columbus arrived.

As Columbus and his crew continued navigate the seas of the Caribbean, they discovered that the indigenous Taínos inhabited what is called Jamaica, Hispaniola (Dominican Republic and Haiti), Puerto Rico, Virgin Islands, and Cuba. Repetitively, Columbus followed the discovery by remarking in his journals, "The Taínos were physically strong, but timid and easily ordered about" (Higman, 2011, p. 62). However, most importantly to him, he recognized a profit center that included fertile soil, timber and minerals. His profit-centered assessment of the islands was a perspective that quickly emanated throughout West Europe. The profit center perspective became the source of long-term crisis and chaos throughout the Caribbean.

Seeking to profit from his discovery, Columbus and his men used the threat of weapons to exploit the strength and skill of the Taínos (Higman, 2011). An example is the extraction of gold. Taíno boys were ordered to find gold in the rugged terrain of Hispaniola; if they did not return with a "hawks-bill full of gold, their hands were cut off and left to bleed to death" (Sale, 1991, p. 154). By 1495, within three years of Columbus's arrival, Taino revolts in Cuba, Hispaniola, and Jamaica created widespread conflict in which the Spaniards answered with "guns, armored cavalry, and fighting dogs. Many of the Taino leaders were burned alive" (Higman, 2011, p. 65).

Inconceivable methods

Bartolome de Las Casa, the Spanish priest who wrote the first historical account of the Caribbean in 1561—*History of the Indies*—estimated that there were eight million Taínos living in the Caribbean when Columbus arrived in 1492 (Monzote, 2011, p. 83). Barker (2011) argued, "Anthropologists suggests the numbers were much higher, up to 12 million" (p. 34). Las Casa, along with other anthropologists and historians, estimated that as many as three million Taínos lived in Hispaniola and 600,000 for each Jamaica and Puerto Rico (Barker, 2011, p. 34). However, Las Casa was also the first to report a strategic genocide of the indigenous cultures throughout the region, he stated, "There were 60,000 people living on this island when I arrived in 1508, over three million people had perished from war, slavery and the mines. Who in future generations will believe this?" (Vickery, 1998, p. 343)

Tragically, depopulating the islands through violent methods seems to be have been a strategic act of preparation. Two years after Columbus had arrived at Hispaniola, the decline in population indicates one of the most horrific events in human history. Starting in 1496, the population size on Hispaniola began to decrease by 50% each year (Higman, 2011). By 1518, twenty-four years after Columbus arrived, only 11,000 Taínos remained on the island; less than 300 lived on the island in 1570 (Higman, 2011). Wolf (2010) referred to the population decline in the Caribbean as "the great dying" (p. 133). Sauer (1966) suggested that the Indian population on Hispaniola numbered in the millions when Columbus arrived in 1492; "by the end of the 1520s only insignificant numbers survived" (p. 65).

Was it a coincidence that the population decline on Hispaniola replicated a pattern throughout the Caribbean? Las Casa was so disturbed by the gruesome cruelty that he witnessed that he renounced his priestly vows to the Spanish crown to defend the defenseless culture. Higman (2011) suggests that the Taino population decline was the result of an economic strategy with "indigenous genocide as the outcome" (p. 77).

Establishing profit centers, irrespective of costs

There is sufficient support for the notion that the catastrophic population decline of indigenous peoples was strategic. As Columbus recognized in his journals, the region had all the components to establish a significant profit center (Higman, 2011). However, since the Taínos were unwilling to serve as a Spanish labor force, they revolted in opposition. The Spanish then turned to the inconceivable, they used the Taínos vulnerability to disease as a weapon. Kohn (2008) suggests that the population decline was the result of infectious diseases, especially small pox. Taylor (2002) argued that it was common practice for all Western European nations to use the spread of disease to establish their territory. He references letters between two military commanders, General Jeffery Amherst and Colonel Henry Bouquet. The letters "explicitly advocate the idea of using smallpox-infested blankets to kill Indians" (Taylor, 2002, p. 40).[2] Following the orders of his commanders, William Trent, a solider in the Spanish army, responded, "We gave them two blankets and a handkerchief infected with Smallpox. I hope it will have the desired effect" (as cited in Taylor, 2002, p. 41).

Following the example of the Spanish, the French also devised a strategic plan to establish a Caribbean profit center. Utilizing the same strategy to depopulate any people group unwilling to be enslaved, the Monarchy published a document called the *Code Noir* (1685). King Louis began his treatise with a statement that reinforced his colonial intentions to depopulate the seized islands in order to maximize profits.

> I   We charge all our officers to evict from our islands all the Jews who have established their residence there, who we order, as to the declared enemies, to leave within three months of the publication date of these edicts or face confiscation of body and property.
>
> (Dubois, 2006, p. 50)

The removal of all population impediments to create capitalistic success is the first tenet of the *Code Noir*. However, it seems to be aligned with the objectives of other imperialistic nations in the Caribbean. When Ferdinand

and Isabella accepted the surrender of the indigenous people of Granada in 1492, their first order was to expel any and all people of Jewish descent (Higman, 2011). Portugal followed suit in the sixteenth century by evicting Jewish prospectors from Barbados when they claimed the island (Palmie & Francisco, 2011). The pattern seems to suggest that profit is paramount, no matter the cost to human lives or long-term consequence to the region.

According to the edicts of Western European monarchies, established cultures were evicted from their territories, millions of indigenous people were violently extinguished, and islands were illegally taken in hostile take overs; therefore, a strategy of depopulation seemed to be the method of growth (Higman, 2011). Further validating the presence of depopulation, the strategy was replicated throughout the region during the encounter era in order to establish profit centers. Although the Encounter Era is defined by Spain's strategies of brutality, economic advantage was firmly imbedded into the foundation of the region, a component that seems applicable to the current reality in the Caribbean.

Are the events from the Encounter Era relevant to today's reality?

Todays' Caribbean possesses characteristics that seem to indicate a direct correlation to the violent events in the Encounter Era (Gmelch, 2012). When Columbus and the Spanish violently disrupted the peace of an indigenous culture to establish a profit center through acts of violence, exploitation, cruelty, resource extraction, and dehumanization; did they set in motion patterns of behavior that affect the present reality in the Caribbean? The most current report from the United Nations Office of Drugs and Crime in the Caribbean report the following statistics (UNODC, 2007, pp. 7–13).

- Murder rates in the Caribbean—at 30 per 100,000 population annually— are higher than for any other region of the world and have risen in recent years for many of the region's countries.
- Crime is arguably the number one social issue for much of the Caribbean, with its only serious rival being economic development (see World Bank, 2005a).
- Regional victimization survey revealed that 48% of adolescent girls' sexual initiation was "forced" or "somewhat forced" in nine Caribbean countries (Halcon et al., 2003).
- Three of the top ten recorded rape rates in the world occur in the Caribbean.

Based on the findings from the UNODC (2007), it seems plausible to suggest that the violent conditions that defined the reality of life for the indigenous cultures of the Caribbean form a continuum to today's reality.[3]

Colonial Period (1501–1945): intentional inconceivability

> The Spanish in the Caribbean had transformed themselves from guests into hosts by exterminating the indigenous population and replacing it with an extraneous, racially alien labor force violently—as well as profitably—extracted from another continent.
>
> (Mintz, 1966, p. 918)

Through a strategic agenda to depopulate, the islands of the Caribbean were prepared to become a strategic profit center for Western Europe. After Columbus violently forced the Taínos to extract the gold from the islands, the region was transformed into agricultural states. However, to plant, produce, and earn a profit required capital investment and the establishment of a plantation colony. In order to generate a return on the investment, the enterprise required an outside labor force. As Palmie (2011) has argued, the Western European investors had a goal to "transplant people for a profit" (p. 132).

The first shipment of African slaves arrived in Hispaniola in 1501 (Morgan, 2011), thus "sugar and slavery [in the Caribbean] became the investor's dream" (Beckles, 1989, p. 208). Twelve years later, there were thirty-four sugar mills on the island, with the owner of the largest sugar mill being Diego Columbus, Christopher Columbus's son. In twelve years, the population of Africans on Hispaniola led the Spanish scribe Oviedo (1546) to state, "as a result of the sugar factories, the land seems an effigy or an image to Ethiopia itself" (Guitar, 2011, p. 117). Aimé Césaire (1950), the Martinique author who introduced the notion of *negritude*, referenced the violently displaced Africans when he suggested

> [t]he men they took away knew how to build houses, govern empires, erect cities, cultivate fields, mine for metals, weave cotton, and forge steel. Their religion had its own beauty, based on mystical connections with the founder of the city. Their customs were pleasing, built on unity, kindness, and respect for age. No coercion, only mutual assistance, the joy of living, a free acceptance of discipline.
>
> (p. 7)

From 1501 to 1870, Morgan (2011) estimated that 5.75 million Africans were violently removed from their cultures and shipped to Western European colonies in the Caribbean. The population size of Africans in the Caribbean in the year 1700 was equivalent to the indigenous population size when Columbus stepped off the ship in 1492. In a matter of 200 years, a "for profit" enterprise extinguished eight million indigenous people and replaced them with eight million violently displaced Africans.

As the first shipments of sugar reached the Spanish city of Seville, which meant that investors were profiting, the French, British and Dutch took notice and forcibly established colonies throughout the Caribbean, though none of them dared to tread on the well-armed and fortified Spanish territories for over 100 years (Palmie, 2011). As a result, the French, British, and Dutch initially settled in the Eastern Caribbean, which is called the Lesser Antilles—each of the respective countries turned to Africa to violently manufacture a labor force.

After a comprehensive analysis of the colonial period, the question that lingers is, "Was the human suffering worth a spoonful of sugar in a cup of tea, a bottle of spirits in a pub, or an increase in profit on the bottom line?" As the colonial period was coming to a close, Césaire (1950) wrote in his renowned discourse on colonialism that the Africans in the Caribbean are "the only class of people that still have a universal mission, because it suffers in the flesh from all the wrong doings of history, from all the universal wrongs" (p. 78).

The violent and economically based chaos initiated by Columbus in the region, resulted in one of the most catastrophic periods in human history. Although the United States honors Columbus with a federal holiday, my observation has been that the residents of the Caribbean legitimately view him in the same light as Adolph Hitler.

Are the events from the Colonial Period relevant to today's reality?

Tragically, the continuum of escalating violence continued throughout the Colonial Period, which equates to 453 consecutive years of enslavement, brutality, cultural conditioning, and dehumanization when combined with the Encounter Era.[4] Gmelch (2012) suggests that each of the conditions serve as sources to the current socioeconomic crisis in the Caribbean. However, two components that were firmly established in the Colonial period remain socioeconomic inhibitors to the cultures in the Caribbean—(1) a profit center for foreigners and (2) a labor force to secure profit.

Although billions of dollars have been expended constructing hotels throughout the region, "two-thirds of the hotel rooms in the region are foreign owned, and the tour companies who arrange visitor's activities are often foreign owned" (Gmelch, 2012, p. 10). In spite of twenty-five million visitors and $49 billion tourist dollars injected into the region in 2013, the African culture in the Caribbean has consistently remained as one of the five poorest cultures in the world (Turner, 2014). A significant reason for the high poverty rate, in contrast to the enormous amount of money spent by tourists, is the amount of money that annually leaves the region— foreign corporations removed 70% of all money spent in the region by tourists in 2013 (Gmelch, 2012). Replicating the imperialistic structure of the colonial period, the Caribbean remains a *profit center* for foreign national corporations.

Further, in order to utilize the *profit center* model established by the imperialistic countries, a *labor force* remains a requirement to secure a profit for the foreign corporations. The *labor force*, which is mainly comprised from the cultures in the Caribbean, seems troubled by the reality of colonialism in their current lives.

Today some West Indians are seeing features of the colonial situation res-
urrected by tourism. Locals are denied access to their own beaches, the
best jobs go to non-nationals or those with the lightest skin, and humble
service roles and low-wage jobs predominate in the tourism sector.

(Gmelch, 2012, p. 12)

Throughout the region there are estimated 4.6 million people who fill the
low-wage jobs in the tourism sector (Pentelow & Scott, 2011). For many
foreign corporations those people are the smiling faces of profit in the Caribbean. To maintain a profit, those same people are trained to consistently
reflect Bob Marley's anthem for the region, "Everting gonna be alright."
However, once the workers leave the lavish environment of their respective
resorts, "everting" is not alright. The reality of their lives is reduced to daily
survival and hardship. The *labor force and profit center* are current realities that
further condition the culture to be reliant and subservient to outside forces.

Decolonized Period (1945–1980): continuum of disorder

Decolonization, which sets out to change the order of the world is, obvi-
ously, a programme of complete disorder.

(Fanon, 1990, p. 27)

When World War II ended in 1945, only three islands in the Caribbean were
independent: Dominican Republic, Haiti, and Cuba. In the next thirty years
(1945–1980), which is defined as the decolonization period, thirteen islands
transitioned into sovereign nations. Although many of the islands had been
colonies for over 400 years, a few chose to negotiate a unique status with
their colonizers, while seven others remained colonies (Table 3.1).

The two largest islands, Cuba and the Dominican Republic/Haiti, had
contentious and violent pathways to achieve sovereign nation status; however,
the other thirteen islands transitioned into sovereignty with little conflict
(Higman, 2011, p. 266). In light of hundreds of years of brutal violence, the
calm ironic transition seemed to be the result of two factors. First, Cuba, the
Dominican Republic and Haiti all suffered through violent labor rebellions,
revolutions, dictators, and political assassinations in their quest for independence. However, the United States was beginning to establish its hegemonic
position in the region and "clearly compromised their [Cuba, Dominican
Republic and Haiti] sovereignty in economic, political, and military terms"
(MacPherson, 2011, p. 475). In spite of their own labor rebellions in the
1930s, it seems the other nations were weary of violence and chose an alternative pathway to sovereignty status (Table 3.1).

The second factor in the clam transition to sovereignty, the French,
British, Dutch, and Spanish colonizers devalued their Caribbean assets and no
longer included them in their global agenda (Higman, 2011). Four hundred
and fifty-three years of resource extraction depleted the region of any natural

Table 3.1 The current status of former Caribbean colonies: the crisis and chaos in the Caribbean

Territory	Colonizing country	Current status	Current governance	Year of independence
Jamaica	United Kingdom	Independent	Self	1962
Trinidad and Tobago	United Kingdom	Independent	Self	1962
Barbados	United Kingdom	Independent	Self	1966
Grenada	United Kingdom	Independent	Self	1978
Dominica	United Kingdom	Independent	Self	1979
St. Lucia	United Kingdom	Independent	Self	1981
Antigua & Barbuda	United Kingdom	Independent	Self	1983
St. Kitts & Nevis	United Kingdom	Independent	Self	1979
St. Vincent	United Kingdom	Independent	Self	1966
Guyana	United Kingdom	Independent	Self	1962
Bahamas	United Kingdom	Independent	Self	1973
Belize	United Kingdom	Independent	Self	1981
Suriname	Dutch	Independent	Self	1975
Guadeloupe	France	Decolonized	Overseas French Dept.	1946
Guyane	France	Decolonized	Overseas region	1983
Martinique	France	Decolonized	Overseas region	1983
Aruba	Denmark	Decolonized	Partner in Kingdom of Netherlands	1954
Netherlands Antilles	Denmark	Decolonized	Partner in Kingdom of Netherlands	1954
Puerto Rico	United States	Decolonized	Commonwealth	1952
Anguilla	United Kingdom	Colonized	United Kingdom	2002
Montserrat	United Kingdom	Colonized	United Kingdom	2002
Turks & Caicos	United Kingdom	Colonized	United Kingdom	2002
Bermuda	United Kingdom	Colonized	United Kingdom	2002
Cayman Islands	United Kingdom	Colonized	United Kingdom	2002
British Virgin Islands	United Kingdom	Colonized	United Kingdom	2002
U.S. Virgin Islands	United States	Colonized	United States	1954

Source: IMF; MacPherson, A., (2011). *The Caribbean: A History of the region and its peoples: Toward decolonization.*

Note

Cuba and Hispaniola (Dominican Republic and Haiti) are not included since their decolonization/liberation took place outside the Decolonization Period. They each became free nations in 1865, 1804, and 1898 respectively.

resources of value. As a result, the imperial nations saw no value in fighting to maintain their colonies in the Caribbean; they were eager to rid themselves of a horrid past and the possibility of a contentious future.

Although the imperial nations violently removed the Africans from their homeland, expunged their sense of self, and reconstituted their identity; those same nations abandoned their enslaved work force on isolated and resource depleted islands. Decolonization is often associated with freedom, sovereignty, and independence. For the sovereign nations of the Caribbean, decolonization has included struggling economies, high crime rates, poverty, tense international relations, and repetitious crisis. MacPherson (2011) characterizes the decolonization period in the Caribbean when she states, "None of the patterns of decolonization has solved the problems that the peoples of the Caribbean faced as inheritors of a brutal 500-year history" (p. 488). Although the islands of the Caribbean were no longer considered an imperialistic asset, the decolonization period did not severe the ties of dependency nor free the Africans in the Caribbean from crisis.

Are the events from the Decolonized Period relevant to today's reality?

The transition from colonial oppression to sovereign status for the nations of the Caribbean prompted a regional and global celebration. Every year after, each of the respective nations have annually celebrated their Independence Day celebrations. Due to the high levels of migration from the region, enthusiastic Independence Day celebrations take place concurrently in cities like New York, Toronto, Atlanta, Miami, and London.[5] However, the current level of violence in the region taints many of the celebrations with an invasive reality—signatures on a document cannot mandate an instant shift in patterns of behavior.[6] The expectation that signed documents of independence would immediately reverse the effects of 500 years of conditioned violence were false. The continuum of violence initiated in the Encounter Era traversed through the Colonial Period, the Decolonization Period, and remains a current reality.

Developmental Period (1955–1982): forfeited independence

> In the Caribbean, the spirit of self-reliance is being systematically destroyed as we keep looking for fairy godmothers and godfathers to hold our hands and lead us to the promised land.
>
> (Girvan (1998), as cited in Randall & Mount, 1998, p. 176)

Five hundred years as an agricultural base for Western Europe, coupled with the emergence of the industrializing United States, shaped the Caribbean into a single-source economy (International Monetary Fund, 2008). With the advent of freedom, the region recognized the need to develop other industries to become globally relevant to ensure a sustainable future;

however, five centuries as an agro-economy meant a lack of infrastructure to facilitate alternative industries. As a result, Jamaica, Trinidad, St. Lucia, Puerto Rico, and Cuba expanded their economic sphere by developing a public sector through international loans, an errant decision that would reinforce the region's high level of dependency (International Monetary Fund, 2008).

Developing the essential public sectors of communication, education, public works and health seemed to be the economic priority all through the 1960s and 1970s (Higman, 2011). Enabled by the development of infrastructure, the industry sector experienced rapid growth—bauxite and coffee in Jamaica; oil and asphalt in Trinidad; tobacco, copper, and lead in Cuba; pharmaceuticals in Puerto Rico; and limestone in the Dominican Republic became sources of revenue and staples in the region (Table 3.2). Meanwhile, the inability or failure to collect on revenue resulted in unmanageable public debt and destabilized economies throughout the region (Erisman, 2003). Borrowing from foreign countries in order to sufficiently develop new sustainable industries seemed to be a pathway to independence, but the errant strategy ignited a migration crisis that remains a current source of socio-economic crisis (Erisman, 2003; Higman, 2011).

Are the events from the Developmental Period relevant to today's reality?

The collective decisions in the development period fortified dependency and created high levels of poverty, which in turn stimulated a migration crisis that affects the current reality of life in the region. Erisman (2003) suggested, "poverty and unemployment fuel migration, and the Caribbean has the highest percentage of migrants of any world region" (p. 173). The scope of the debilitating migration crisis is revealed in Kristen McCabe's report from The Migration Policy Institute (2016).

- There are 6.8 million self-identified members of the Caribbean diaspora residing in the United States.
- In the 2011 Census of England and Wales, nearly 1.1 million people indicated they were of Caribbean descent—(2011 Census: Ethic Group, England and Wales).
- Nearly 700,000 people who claim Caribbean descent live in Canada. The Caribbean population in Canada is growing at a faster rate (11%) than the Canadian population growth rate (4%)—(www.statcan.gc.ca, February 2016).
- The Caribbean-born population in the United States has increased more than seventeen-fold over the past fifty years.
- Over 90% of the Caribbean immigrants are from Cuba, the Dominican Republic, Jamaica, Haiti, Trinidad and Tobago.
- Nearly four of every ten immigrants in Florida were born in the Caribbean.

Based on McCabe's findings, over 25% of Caribbean born people now live abroad, compared to 1.2% of Americans who live abroad and 0.75% of Brazilians who live abroad (Focus-Migration, 2016).[7] The high migration rate in the Caribbean suggests that a sense of self, sense of place, and realized potential regarding its residents remains destabilized. Thus, the freedom of independence did not stabilize the region, but provided the people with the opportunity to leave behind the debilitating effects of long-term socioeconomic crisis.

Although there were well-intended efforts to place crisis and chaos in the distant past, the outcomes of the development period are contributors to the current socioeconomic crises of dependency, debt, and poverty for the nations of the Caribbean. As with all the preceding historical periods of the region, socioeconomic crisis escalated in the developmental period.

Neoliberal Period (1980–current): exploited outcomes

> Without exception, the neo-liberal model exacerbated rather than eliminated problems of social and economic equity in the Caribbean.
>
> (Randall & Mount, 1998, p. 175)

Due to soaring poverty rates, excessive debt loads, high unemployment rates, and currency devaluation throughout the developmental period, the political powers of the Caribbean sought an alternative economic structure to ease hardship in the region. The neoliberal model selected was a structure designed by developmental agencies in first world nations (Sachs, 1999). Recognizing that the structure was developed around economic liberty and independence, the general consensus in the region was that the structure seemed well suited for the highly dependent Caribbean nations (Harvey, 2005).

The neoliberal model utilizes privatization, deregulation, free trade, and fiscal austerity to remove government impediments from the free markets, a seemingly great fit for the fledging economics in the Caribbean. Thomas Klak (1998), in *Globalization and Neoliberalism: The Caribbean Context*, defined neoliberalism as "a movement toward a more laissez-faire capitalism in the global periphery" (p. 17); however, he was concerned that implementing a "one size fits all" economic model was not "sensitive to the special problems faced by small economies in general, and those of the Caribbean in particular" (p. 17).

Eager to place the region on a pathway toward economic independence, the political powers of the Caribbean confirmed that the opportunity for economic independence outweighed the risks of the neo-liberal structure (Randall & Mount, 1998). After taking the appropriate measures to implement the structure, global leaders praised the progress. The IMF Deputy Managing Director Shigemitsu Sugisaki (International Monetary Fund, 1998) suggested that the independent nations of the Caribbean were progressing toward an economic independence and freedom as a result of the neo-liberal model. However, true independence never materialized. Sugisaki (International Monetary Fund, 2012) later admitted that he was incorrect in his assessment of the Caribbean

Table 3.2 Population: key features of the islands in the Caribbean

Category	For Caribbean
Cumulative population	40 million
Total number of islands	Over 7,000
Number of countries	25
Regional division	*Greater Antilles*: Jamaica, Cuba, Hispaniola (Dominican Republic/Haiti), Puerto Rico. *Lesser Antilles*: U.S. Virgin Islands, British Virgin Islands, Anguilla, St. Martin, St. Barthelemy, Saba, St. Kitts, Nevis, Barbuda, Antiqua, St. Eustatius, Redonda, Montserrat, Guadeloupe, Dominica, Martinique, St. Lucia, St. Vincent, Grenada, Aruba, Curacao, Bonaire.
Indigenous people	Arawaks, Taínos, and Caribs
Diversity	West Indian (Afro-Carib), East Indian, Spanish, French, American (US), Dutch, British, South African, Asian and a remnant of Arawaks and Caribs.
Linguistics	Based on the population, more people speak Spanish in the Caribbean than any other language, followed by French, English, Creole, Patois, Dutch, Haitian, and Papiamento.
Active volcanoes	Montserrat, Grenada, St. Lucia, St. Vincent, and Dominica
Formation	Except for Trinidad, which rests on the tectonic plate of S. America, the islands of the Caribbean were formed through volcanic activity.
Coral reefs	8% of the coral reefs in the world are in the Caribbean. 29% of reefs in the region are threatened due to human activity/marine pollution.

Climate	Tropical, mean temperature throughout the region is 25°C (77°F). Rainfall amounts vary from 16 inches per year in Aruba—200 inches per year in the Blue Mountains of Jamaica. Prevailing northeast trade winds. Hurricane season is June–November.
Agricultural crops	Bananas, Coffee, Sugar, Tobacco
Minerals	Gold, silver, nickel, bauxite, limestone
Rain forests	Dominica, Jamaica, Puerto Rico
Carbon footprint	Per capita emissions (>2.0), highest of any region in the world
Fossil fuels	10% of GDP is expended on fossil fuels to produce energy (except Trinidad).
Further concerns	Elevated sea temperatures are bleaching the coral reefs.
	All the major commercial specifies of fish have been exploited, I.e.: Conch has been listed as endangered.
	Income disparity continues to increase.
	Infrastructure constructed on fossil fuels has suppressed efforts for alternative energy sources.
	National debt ratio is the highest in the world.
	Personal income, GDP, and jobs have the highest percentage of dependency of any region in the world.
	Dependency on foreign nations/institutions is increasing.

Sources: Convention on International trade in endangered species, Millennium Ecosystem Assessment, U.S. Department of Energy, CIA Fact book, World Tourism and Travel Counsel, IMF, World Bank.

by acknowledging that the region's economy was too weak and not capable of reducing "the distressingly high rates of unemployment and poverty." Thus, the region remained mired in socioeconomic crisis.

Exploited opportunity

The failure of the neoliberal model once again accentuated the most common question in the Caribbean, "Why is this happening to us?" When the global economic powers recognized that the Caribbean was delinquent in their debt, vulnerable to the hegemonic powers, and desperate to end the long-term socioeconomic crisis, they pressed the Caribbean nations to adopt the neoliberal model (Klak, 1998). However, the model was not conducive to the size, structure, or underdevelopment of the Caribbean—"the 'perfectly misunderstood' neo-liberal model was imported from the developed world and urged on the region by the international funding agencies" (Randall & Mount, 1998, p. 175). As a result, China, Japan, Western Europe, and the United States exploited the region's financial vulnerability for their own economic gain and became the benefactors in the neoliberal period. Klak (1998) summed up the neo-liberal influence in the Caribbean by stating,

> [t]he region is abjectly dependent, which continues to the present. The Caribbean region is now largely independent from Europe politically, but is still reeling under the historical legacies of dependency on outside authorities, suppliers, markets, and geopolitical agendas.
>
> (p. 6)

The outcomes of higher poverty rates and greater dependency validate Klak's (1998) assessment—the *one size fits all* neo-liberal model was not designed for small economies in the Caribbean. After the short-lived development in the region faded, the neo-liberal structure facilitated a restored dependency that once again saturated the Caribbean in a socio-economic crisis (Schmidt, 2000). The neo-liberal model further fortified the Caribbean as a peripheral region, dependent upon hegemonic nations for its stability (International Monetary Fund, 2012).

Are the events from the Neoliberal Period relevant to today's reality?

The current economic reality substantiates that "the Caribbean never enjoyed any regional or global order built upon the neoliberal reciprocal principle of mutual advantage" (Schmidt, 2000, p. 1). Tragically, five decades after "claimed" independence, the laissez-faire atmosphere has further marginalized the Caribbean, "duplicating the legacies of old and widening gaps in wealth and power between Core and Periphery" (Schmidt, 2000, p. 1). Robert Goddard (2011), the Caribbean historian from Barbados, suggested, "The forces of economic globalization have undermined the autonomy of small states in the Caribbean" (p. 582). Speaking to the current socio-economic reality in the Caribbean, Owen Arthur, the former Prime Minister in Barbados summarized, "The Caribbean now actually finds itself slumped over the bar, drinking the last dregs at the bottom of the glass in the last-chance saloon" (Arthur (2014) as quoted in Bishop, 2015, p. 12). Thus, the present reality for the Afro-Caribs is escalated socioeconomic crisis, a debilitating reality that has been present throughout all five historical eras of the region.

Summation of historical periods

The analysis of the five historical periods in the Caribbean has produced themes that reflect the reality of life consistent throughout each era; profit center, oppression, violence, dependency, underdevelopment, migration, and intensifying hardship. Per the historical account in the Encounter Era, Columbus and the imperialist nations imbedded those themes in the initial conditions of the region. As the analysis progressed, those same themes seemed to be the source of 500 years of escalating crises, yet none of those themes validate the assumed lens of "paradise."

Although the nations of the Caribbean have taken a few steps toward sustainable autonomy, Maingot (2011) argued, "there are more steps to take, given the seriousness of the problems in the region" (p. 534). The historical themes accentuate the *seriousness of the problems in the region* and illuminate the necessity for defining the *steps* out of 500 years of socioeconomic crisis. Further, the events and themes of the historical progression are congruent with my observations as a participant in the socioeconomic crisis that hinders the cultures of the Caribbean.

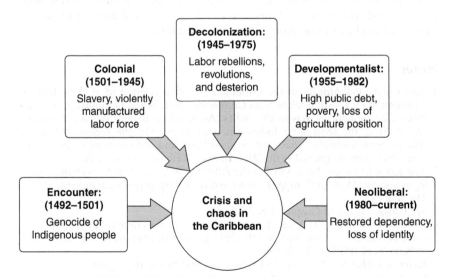

Figure 3.1 Historical periods, events, and positions.

Summary of the historical periods of the Caribbean

- The Encounter Era is defined by the discovery of indigenous cultures, the genocide of the indigenous cultures, and the establishment of a profit center.
- The Colonial Period is marked by the occupation and brutality of the imperialistic nations, a violently manufactured labor force, imperialistic dominance, cultural conditioning, dehumanization, and a collective force of violent oppression.
- The Decolonized Era symbolized independence from long-term imperialistic rule, the abandonment of an enslaved work force on isolated and resource depleted islands, high crime rates, poverty, tense international relations, and repetitious crisis.
- The Development Period represents economic policy and expansion beyond agriculture, high volumes of debt, and high migration rates.
- The Neoliberal Period can be characterized by further exploitation and a restored dependency on the United States, Western Europe, Japan and China.

Key features and diversity of the Caribbean

Based on the cultural and geographical characteristics of the Caribbean, the region remains one of the top tourists destinations in the world. The Caribbean Tourism Quality Index (The Caribbean Tourism Quality Index, 2015) estimated that thirty million tourists in 2014 visited the aquamarine waters, expansive white beaches, volcanic elevations, tropical climate, coral reefs, and bountiful species in the sea. However, the characteristics of the Caribbean go far beyond a beach and a bar, the linguistic and specie diversity of the region establishes the Caribbean as one of the top three culturally diversified regions in the world (International Monetary Fund, 2012). As Table 3.2 illustrates, there is a broad sect of diversity within the Caribbean.

Notes

1 Afro-Caribs and Africans in the Caribbean are often referred to as West Indians. The term West Indian resulted from Columbus' error. When he landed in the Caribbean, he thought he was in the Indies (Asia), which is east. When the mistake was realized, the term West Indies was used to describe the region. When the Africans were violently extracted from their homeland and relocated to the Caribbean, they were designated as the West Indians. Reference Glossary A.
2 The actual letters can be accessed at the following links: www.nativeweb.org/pages/legal/amherst/34_40_305_fn.jpeg   www.nativeweb.org/pages/legal/amherst/34_41_114_fn.jpeg
3 See Chaos Theory in Chapter 4 of this book.
4 Refer to UNODC (2007) for a lens of current reality for crime in the region.
5 Over two million people attended the 2013 Jamaica Independence Day celebration in New York (Phillips, T., 2015).
6 Refer to UNODC (2007, pp. 7–13) for crime statistics in the region.
7 Brazil was utilized as a point of reference due to its political unrest and long-term socio-economic crisis.

References

Arthur, O. (2014). Caribbean Regionalism in the Context of Economic Challenges. *Caribbean Journal of International Relations & Diplomacy*, 2(4): 147–164.

Barker, D. (2011). Geographies of opportunities, geographies of constraint. In S. Palmie, & S. Francisco, (Eds), *The Caribbean: A history of the region and its peoples*. Chicago, IL: University of Chicago Press.

Beckles, H. (1989). *Natural rebels: A social history of enslaved black women in Barbados*. London: Cambridge Press.

Beckles, H., & Shepherd, V. (2004). *Liberties lost: The indigenous Caribbean and slave systems*. Cambridge, U.K.: Cambridge University Press.

Columbus, C., & Toscanelli, P. (2010) [1893]. C. Markham, (ed.). *The journal of Christopher Columbus (During hs first voyage)*. London: Cambridge University Press.

Césaire, A. (1950). *Discourse on colonialism*. New York, NY: Monthly Review Press.

Erisman, M. (2003). International relations. In R. Hillman, & T. D'Agnostino (Eds), *Understanding the Contemporary Caribbean*. Boulder, CO: Lynne Rienner, pp. 161–187.

Fanon, F. (1990). *The wretched of the earth*. London: Penguin Press.

Focus-Migration (2016, January). Retrieved from www.focus-migration.hwwi.de

Girvan, N. (2012, November). Colonialism and neo-colonialism in the Caribbean: An overview. Paper presented at the IV International Seminar Africa, the Caribbean, and Latin America, Kingston, Jamaica. Retrieved from www.normangirvan.info/wp-content/uploads/2013/01/Girvan-St-Vincent-paper.pdf

Gmelch, G. (2012). *Beyond the Smile: The working lives of Caribbean tourism*. Bloomington, IN: Indiana University Press.

Goddard, R. (2011). Tourism, drugs, off-shore finance, and the perils of neo-liberal development. In S. Palmie, & S. Francisco (Eds), *The Caribbean: A history of the region and its peoples*, Chicago, IL: University of Chicago Press, pp. 473–492.

Guitar, L. (2011). Negotiations of conquest. In S. Palmie, & S. Francisco (Eds), *The Caribbean: A history of the region and its peoples*. Chicago, IL: University of Chicago Press.

Harvey, D. (2005). *A brief history of neoliberalism*. New York, NY: Oxford University Press.

Higman, B. (2011). *A concise history of the Caribbean*. New York, NY: Cambridge University Press.

International Monetary Fund (1998, October 8). Regional economic outlook: Western hemisphere. Retrieved from www.imf.org/external/pubs/ft/survey/survey98.htm

International Monetary Fund (2008). The Caribbean: Enhancing economic integration. Retrieved from www.imf.org/external/pubs/ft/dp/2008/dp0802.pdf

International Monetary Fund (2012, April 12). World economic outlook: Western hemisphere, rebuilding strength and flexibility. Retrieved from www.imf.org/external/pubs/ft/reo/2012/whd/eng/pdf/wreo0412.pdf

Klak, T. (1998). *Globalization and neoliberalism: The Caribbean context*. Lanham, MD: Rowan & Littlefield.

Kohn, G. (2008). *Encyclopedia of plague and pestilence: From ancient items to the present* (3rd ed.). New York, NY: Facts of File.

MacPherson, A. (2011). Toward colonization. In S. Palmie, & S. Francisco (Eds), *The Caribbean: A history of the region and its peoples*. Chicago, IL: University of Chicago Press, pp. 473–492.

Maingot, A. (2011). Independence and its aftermath: Suriname, Trinidad, and Jamaica. In S. Palmie, & S. Francisco (Eds), *The Caribbean: A history of the region and its peoples*. Chicago, IL: University of Chicago Press.

McCabe, K. (2016, February). Report from The Migration Policy Institute. Retrieved from www.migrationpolicy.org

Mintz, S. (1966). The Caribbean as a socio-cultural area. Retrieved from www.sidney mintz.net

Monzote, R. (2011). *From rainforest to canefield: An environmental history of Cuba*. Chapel Hill, NC: University of North Carolina Press.

Morgan, K. (2011). *A short history of transatlantic slavery*. New York, NY: Oxford University Press.

Palmie, S., & Francisco, S. (Eds) (2011). *The Caribbean: A history of the region and its peoples*. Chicago, IL: University of Chicago Press.

Pentelow, L., & Scott, D. (2011). Aviation's inclusion in international climate policy regimes: Implications for the Caribbean tourism industry. *Journal of Air Transport Management*, 17: 199–205.

Phillips, T. (2015, August). Timeout New York: Guide to the West Indian parade. Retrieved from www.timeout.com/newyork/west-indian-american-day-carnival-new-york

Randall, S., & Mount, G. (1998). *The Caribbean basin: An international history*. London: Routledge.

Sale, K. (1991). *The conquest of paradise: Christopher Columbus and the Columbian legacy*. New York, NY: Plume.

Sauer, C. (1966). *The early Spanish Main*. Los Angeles, CA: University California Press.

Schmidt, A. (2000). Caribbean lament. [Review of the book *Globalization and neoliberalism: The Caribbean context*]. H-Net Reviews in the Humanities & Social Sciences. Retrieved from www.h-net.org

Taylor, A. (2002). *American colonies,* Vol. I of *Penguin History of the United States*. New York, NY: Penguin Press.

The Caribbean Tourism Quality Index (2015). The resonance report. Retrieved from http://skift.com/wp-content/uploads/2014/11/CaribbeanQualityTourismReport 2015-11.pdf

Turner, R. (2014). Travel and Tourism, Economic Impact 2014, *World Travel and Tourism Council*. Retrieved from www.wttc.org/-/media/files/reports/economic%20 impact%20research/regional%202015/caribbean2014.pdf

UNODC, Report No. 37820: *Crime, Violence, and Development: Trends, Costs, and Policy Options in the Caribbean*. March 2007. Retrieved from www.unodc.org/pdf/ research/Cr_and_Vio_Car_E.pdf

Vickery, P. (1998). *Bartolome de las Casas: Great prophet of the Americas*. Mahwah, NJ: Paulist Press.

Walcott, D. (1984) *Midsummer: XXVII*. New York, NY: Macmillan Press.

Wolf, E. (2010). *Europe and the people without history*. Berkeley, CA: University California Press.

4 An intentional reality

Three lenses of perspective

Strategic outcomes are produced from intentionally designed environments. The three lenses of perspective in this segment will focus on intentional realities that produce strategic outcomes. The first two theoretical lenses will filter the socioeconomic reality in the Caribbean and assess the intent of their outcomes. Based on the reality exposed in the first two lenses, the third lens will expound on an intentional response that facilitates an outcome of sustainable growth. Each of the three lenses will be contrasted to the themes originating in the two preceding segments—my observations as a participant in the reality of life and the historical analysis of the region. It should be noted that the scope of this project is not limited to a comprehensive analysis of the socioeconomic crisis in the Caribbean. This project is committed to identify a path of sustainable growth for the cultures of the Caribbean. All three of the selected lenses speak directly to the objectives of this project—each of the lenses was selected as a point of reference for corroboration or rejection of my biased observations.

To sufficiently analyze intentional realities in the Caribbean, I recognize a need to expand my worldview. Capra and Luisi (2014) suggested that it's easy to establish errant positions through, "a perception (perspective) of reality that is inadequate for dealing with crisis" (p. xi). Acknowledging that my two-decade bond with the African culture could skew my perspective of the socioeconomic crisis in the Caribbean, I broadened my perspective of the crisis through diverse scholarly positions. The diversity includes Caribbean scholars, current theorists, and classical economists from the eighteenth, nineteenth, and twentieth centuries who provide clear measurements for defining the crisis and identifying a pathway out.

This project places significant emphasis on the perspectives of Caribbean scholars. In a strategic effort to establish a comprehensive appraisal of the socioeconomic crisis in the Caribbean and reduce the probability of errant positions, I have utilized the works of Caribbean scholars as a filter of understanding. Although the theoretical scope of this project extends beyond the works by Caribbean scholars, I have highlighted the voice of Afro-Carib scholars in order to develop a relevant course of meaning to analyze the relationship between creative practice and socioeconomic crisis in the Caribbean.

To address the qualitative nature of the project, I begin by stating my biased positions.

1   The perpetual socioeconomic conditions in the Caribbean seem to indicate that implemented socioeconomic polices derived from outside the region have not been effective; therefore, economic models developed for established cultures may be ineffective for cultures that have been displaced through violence and oppression.
2   Cultures displaced through an act of imperialistic violence and oppression seem to have core values that reflect their ontology.
3   Marxism, socialism, communism, and capitalism are all imperfect socioeconomic models that have historical records of atrocity and oppression.
4   The planet as a whole is a living, self-regulating system, where creativity is the driving force of self-regeneration and authentic identity.
5   Creative practice is an essential means to move beyond existing conditions of reality.

Seeking a broad command of comparative political theory, international relations, socioeconomic structures, cultural crisis, models of sustainability, and theories of creative practice, I have strategically selected a group of multidisciplinary scholarly works for analysis. Research from economists, sociologists, ecologists, and cognitionists contributes to a deep understanding of socioeconomic crisis and creative practice as a force of change. Furthermore, this project evaluates the selected works in order to determine their relevance to the central question of this project, "What is the relationship between creative practice and the socioeconomic crisis in the Caribbean?"

Caribbean scholars: the voice from within

To sufficiently establish meaning regarding the relationship between creative practice and socioeconomic crisis in the Caribbean, this project will highlight the voice and positions of Caribbean scholars, which includes three Nobel Laureates, a Secretary General of the Association of Caribbean States, a member of the United Nations Committee on Development, a chief economist for Ghana, a Carib-French psychiatrist, and a renowned Caribbean playwright. Although their positions are referenced in all three theoretical lenses that follow, their positionality is vital to the theoretical relevance to this project. Brief profiles for each of the Caribbean scholars included in this project are found in Appendix A.

Other notable scholars

The following Caribbean scholars are also referenced in this project: Havelock Brewster (Guyana); William Demas (Trinidad and Tobago); Alister McIntyre (Grenada); Vidiadhar Naipaul (Trinidad and Tobago); Terrance

Farrell (Trinidad and Tobago); Frantz Fanon (Martinique); Edouard Glissant (Martinique); Brian Meeks (Jamaica); and Joan Purcell (Grenada). Furthermore, this project strategically includes scholars that speak directly to the Caribbean, yet are not indigenous to the region. They are: Albert Memmi (Tunisia), Werner Zips (Germany), Karen Olwig (Denmark), Pope Atkins (United States), Peter Jacques (United States), James Scott (United States), Keith Negus (United Kingdom), and Michael Pickering (United Kingdom).

Theoretical lens I: going for the goods—the dark side of capitalism

My daily observations as a participant in Caribbean life provoked me to question accepted realities. An example would be agriculture—since the Caribbean has been an agricultural base for much of the world for 500 years, why has Eric Traille's village in York Castle, Jamaica suffered through extreme hardship since the island received its independence in 1962?[1] Eric was conditioned to farm, his community was conditioned to be an agricultural base, yet the Caribbean currently imports more food per capita than any region in the world (Sanders, 2014).[2] Recognizing that Eric's plight is reflective of many people throughout the region, how did this radical shift take place in less than sixty years? Perplexing realities such as agriculture, education, economic structures, and personal growth motivated me to seek answers beyond my biased observations. The following lens is an effort to understand "why" extreme hardship remains a reality for nearly forty million people in the Caribbean.

External control

Reaching for a contextual reality in the Caribbean, the Jamaican economist Girvan (2012) opened the *Fourth International Seminar of Africa and the Caribbean* in November of 2012, by stating,

> The contemporary Caribbean is one of the most politically fragmented regions for its size on earth; and one with the strongest remaining colonial presence. Political divisions and external control are major blocs to the consolidation of a Caribbean identity and the charting of an independent course of development in the interest of Caribbean peoples. They undermine the fragmented nationalism, and the persuasive epistemological dependency, that is characteristic of the regional consciousness. This situation is a direct consequence of the region's five-century long history as area rivalry among, and colonisation by, external powers. Political decolonisation of Caribbean countries is incomplete; indeed it has come to a virtual standstill.
>
> (2012, p. 1)

Girvan's firsthand assessment of the region, which includes descriptive terms such as, *external control, major blocs, identity, dependence, development, consequence,* and *standstill* serves as a theoretical guide for inquiry in this project. There-fore, the first lens in this project will be an expansion on Girvan's assessment of the region through the utilization of hegemonic, development, and under-development theories. Further, it should be noted that the economic prin-ciples implemented throughout the decolonizing era are the focus of analysis in this segment, however; the residual effects are a source of the current socioeconomic crisis in the region.

An intimidating power: hegemonic theory

> By dependence, I mean the relations between centres and the periphery whereby a country is subjected to decisions taken in the centres, not only economic matters, but also in matters of politics and strategy for domestic and foreign policies. The consequence is that due to exterior pressure the peripheral country cannot decide autonomously what it should do or cease doing.
>
> (Prebisch, 1980, p. 25)

The socioeconomic positions of Girvan, Chilcote, Prebisch, and James serve as points of reference in this project. Acknowledging that many of their socioeconomic paradigms were constructed utilizing the transitions from imperialism to capitalism or capitalism to socialism, their application and relevance have historical significance concerning the longstanding hardship endured by the African culture in the Caribbean.

The Argentinian economist Prebisch (1951) theorized that the world was divided into two distinct divisions, a *center* and a *periphery* (Chilcote, 1984, p. 23). He defined the *center* as the industrialized *center* and the *periphery* as an underdeveloped necessity (Prebisch, 1951, p. 21). As his position evolved, he recognized that the relationship that existed between the *center* and *periphery* could be healthy and beneficial for both sides only for a short period of time. Once the relationship matured, the benefit for the *periphery* would quickly wane due to the emergence of *unequal exchange* (Chilcote, 1984).

A *center/periphery* socioeconomic structure is developed through a strategic trade imbalance (or *unequal exchange*). Prebisch (1951) suggested that the *center* or industrialized core is created through a hegemonic position. Through the use of the hegemony, the *center* strategically develops the socioeconomic order by exploiting two significant economic factors, dependency and limita-tion. Once achieved, the *periphery* defines the *center* as their means of survival (dependency), while the *center* obtains from the *periphery* the maximum limits of agriculture and raw materials (limitation). Therefore, as the *periphery* is bound to a status quo position of dependency, the *center* establishes a trajec-tory of growth through accumulation, development, and industrialized trade (Prebisch, 1951). Thus, the periphery remains static, while the center grows.

When dominant cultures formulate hegemony through a position of intim-idating power, the dominance becomes the accepted source of socioeconomic and geo-political order in the periphery (Jacques, 2015). The results of the *center/periphery* relationship are most evident in the contrast of the socio-economic structures. Chilcote (1984) argued that the reality of the oppressive relationship forced the *periphery* to suffer through a delay of "technology, means of consumption, cultural forms, and ideologies" (p. 25). Prebisch (1951) suggested the suffrage of the *periphery* reached beyond a economic model and influenced the social structures—when a social structure "permits income to concentrate in the hands of the people who own and control the majority of the means of production and that regulates a large part of the working population to low levels of productivity" (Chilcote, 1984, p. 25), the result is dependency and long-term strain in the periphery.

Since this project is focused on the African culture in the Caribbean, it should be noted that the *center/periphery* relationship defined in this section seems to characterize the dependency and struggle throughout the region. In order for Western Europe to maintain a trajectory of growth, they needed to secure the resources in the Caribbean at a fixed and reduced price. However, to keep the Caribbean from developing into a global competitor they utilized their hegemonic position to establish a relationship of dependency. Chilcote's (1984) assessment suggests that the hegemonic position strategically obstructed the socioeconomic development of the Caribbean.

Girvan and Girvan (1973) suggests that the *center/periphery* relationships originated in the Caribbean in the early 1960s, which is when the majority of the Caribbean nations began the process of decolonization. Characterizing the scope of the relationships, Girvan stated, "At that time it (center/periphery) came to be seen as the dominant feature of the structure and functioning of Caribbean economies" (Girvan & Girvan, 1973, p. 4). Randall and Mount (1998) suggested there are many historical examples of such hegemony—Cuba, Puerto Rico, Guam, Jamaica, and the Philippines. Each of the examples demonstrates consistent socioeconomic outcomes of dependency, oppression, and cultural conditioning.

Observing the outcomes of intimidating power

The oppressive insertion of hegemonic power seems to explain why the Rastaman from Jamaica, who sought to frighten me from Jamaica, was so angered by my presence. He viewed me as another wave of intimidating power, an enforcer of colonial oppression. Although his perspective caused him to falsely judge me, his reality motivated him to act. His lens of reality has been tempered by intimidating power throughout his life—is he to blame for his lens? Further, is it valid to assume that the reality of intimidating power will subtly fade away and be replaced by peace and harmony? The current socioeconomic reality in the region suggests that hegemonic power does not subtly fade over time. Declarations of independence were signed throughout the region in the 1960s, yet fifty years later crime escalates and the Caribbean remains one of the five poorest cultures in the world (Turner, 2014), while foreign governments and corporations remove 70% of all money spent in the region (Gmelch, 2012). Just as hegemonic powers have strategically asserted their oppressive power in the Caribbean, it seems that independence and sustainable growth are contingent on intentionality, not a false hope of subtle transition.

Growth strategy: develop me—underdevelop you

> At the center, growth is development—in the periphery, growth is not development. Growth in the periphery, based on integration into the world market, is development of underdevelopment.
>
> (Amin, 1974, p. 18)

Neither Prebisch, nor Chilcote, nor Rodney used the term *deception* when expanding on their *development/underdevelopment* theories; however, many of their historical references of *development/underdevelopment* identify an illusion of autonomy propagated in the *center*. Chilcote (1984) suggested that while fledgling nations are legitimately eager to create their independence and identity, hegemonic nations exploit the vulnerability in the *periphery* by offering a development pathway to autonomy that is rooted in a fundamental falsehood. Prebisch (1980) expanded on the consequence for the *peripheral* nations when they enter into developmental trade agreements that are generated through a fundamental falsehood, he stated, "there is an exterior pressure on the peripheral country, which cannot decide autonomously what it should do or cease doing" (p. 25). Rodney (1972) characterized the relationship between *development/underdevelopment* countries as a relationship of knowing and unknowing exploitation (p. 37).

Assessments of socioeconomic development are not limited to the varied positions of economists; critical assessments of development and underdevelopment have been generated through many disciplines of research and thought. Philosophers such as Socrates, Pascal, and Strauss have all suggested that models of development within industrialized nations emanated through the filter of deception. Socrates was convinced that citizens of respective cultures had to be deceived into believing that social classes were a divine order in the ideal city (Allen, 2006). Likewise, Pascal believed those who used oppression as a method of development strategically deceived the oppressed in order to perpetuate the *center's* abundance.

> The wisest of legislators used to say that men must often be deceived for their own good.... The truth about the usurpation [of justice by force] must not be made apparent; it came about originally without reason and has been made reasonable. We must see that it is regarded as authentic and eternal, and its origins must be hidden if we do not want it soon to end.
>
> (Pascal, 1966, p. 46)

Strauss (1978) pressed for a collective resistance from the masses when he suggested that a legislative objective of a "good city" was not possible without deception. He wrote, "The good city is not possible without a fundamental falsehood; it cannot exist in the element of truth, of nature" (p. 102).

When the majority of the Caribbean nations were "allowed" to claim their sovereign independence throughout the 1960s, they desired *a good city*, one that would develop through the steps of autonomy. However, within a decade of independence the hegemonic nations strategically secured the agriculture and raw materials of the island nations by formulating a protected price structure. An example of the *development/underdevelopment* strategy is the Lome Convention, signed in 1975 by sixteen independent Caribbean nations (Laaksonen, Maki-Franti, & Virolainen, 2010).[3] Placing five centuries of slavery and oppression behind them, the Caribbean nations eagerly agreed to supply the United Kingdom with agriculture and raw materials at protected prices (Shay, Robinson, & Cashin, 2006). In return, the sixteen fledging island nations received a preferential trade position in order to develop an autonomous socioeconomic structure. Yet, the economic structure that the island nations considered an asset of development was actually a manipulated strategy to ensure *underdevelopment*—an illusion of a good city (Girvan & Girvan, 1973).

As with many Caribbean scholars throughout the decolonization period, Girvan (1973) and Walcott (1969) referenced the strategic underdevelopment of the Caribbean. Girvan (1973) spoke about the outcomes of *underdevelopment* and the fundamental falsehoods regarding the preference agreements when he stated, "the effect of preferences was to act as a negative incentive towards the expansion of a West Indian manufacturing industry" (p. 5). Walcott (1969) utilized his poetry to reflect on the devastating effects of *underdevelopment* in the Caribbean, "There is nowhere to go. You'd better go" (p. 92). Walcott is suggesting that periphery nations cannot provide an environment of personal growth, only oppressive routine; therefore, you better leave for a place that facilities personal growth.

Just as Prebisch (1951), Chilcote (1984), and Amin (1974) theorized, developing cultures construct the *center* by exploiting the agriculture and raw materials in the *periphery* (Chilcote, 1984). Maintaining the growth trajectory for the industrialized *center* requires two key components, elevated production and increased exports (Prebisch, 1951). Since industrial production is completely dependent upon materials to make products, materials are an essential source of growth (Chilcote, 1984). Without materials, which lead to production, the industrialized nations have significantly limited their ability to export for profit. Limiting the ability to export negates the factors of growth.

To satisfy their growth criteria, the United Kingdom (*center*) had to strategically fix prices for agriculture and raw materials in the Caribbean (*periphery*) to maintain their growth trajectory (Girvan & Girvan, 1973). With the preference agreement implemented, the economic theory of supply and demand became a reality—as the demand for products made in the United Kingdom increased, the prices of their products also increased. Yet while the United Kingdom's exports to emerging nations remained on a growth trajectory, the prices of the agriculture and raw materials needed for growth remained static in the *periphery*.

Founded on a baseline of deception, the imperialistic cultures of the *center* thrived in growth throughout the developmental and neo-liberal periods of the Caribbean, while the *periphery* (Caribbean) was forced to standstill in a mode of underdevelopment (Girvan & Girvan, 1973). To maintain a growth trajectory, the imperialistic *center* required a dependent *periphery*. In turn, the strategy the *center* employed to secure dependency in the Caribbean was *underdevelopment* (Chilcote, 1984). Sunkel and Girvan (1973) suggested that *development/underdevelopment* is a strategic and concerted process. Based on the referenced socio-economic positions of Prebisch, Girvan, Chilcote, Sunkel and Amin, the imperialistic *center* strategically developed their respective cultures while concurrently suppressing development in the *periphery* (Caribbean). Ultimately, the current socio-economic conditions in the Caribbean are a consequence of the imperialistic strategy, which would award validity to the *development/underdevelopment* theories of Girvan (1973), Chilcote (1984), Prebisch (1951), and Rodney (1972).

Observing the outcomes of underdevelopment

Underdevelopment has had a significant impact on the reality of life in the Caribbean, possibly none greater than in the education sector. When grandparents, parents, and students filled my office in Jamaica hoping to enroll their respective student in the school, I routinely observed expressions of hopelessness.[4] Their image of the "good city" legitimately included an education for all those in the *city*. When the people realized that an education at a public high school was reserved only for a select few, their reality of the *good city* was shattered, forcing them to embrace hopelessness and anger. Henke (2001) expounded on this reality when he suggested:

> West Indian families see education as the most promising way to a better life. Because of the relative lack of placement opportunities (in many countries there is only a limited number of available places in secondary schools) and the stiff competition among students for high school, education is regarded as a privilege.
>
> (p. 133)

The shattering of the *good city* or the broken *promise of a better life* seems to be illuminated when the hope of self-growth and potential are perceived as unattainable.

Due to underdevelopment, education budgets throughout the Caribbean have been reduced to the bare minimum, limiting the number of schools, resources, and teachers (UNICEF, 2013). Further, it seems plausible that underdevelopment in the education sector has contributed to high crime rates. When generations of children are forced to stop their education prior to high school,[5] should anyone be surprised that the Caribbean possesses the highest crime rate of any region in the world (World Health Organization, 2014)? Underdevelopment has limited the educational opportunities for generations of people in the Caribbean, which has progressively extracted the hope of personal growth.

Summation of lens I: going for the goods—the dark side of capitalism

Motivated by profit, the Western European Nations established a hegemonic position throughout in the Caribbean. In order to do so, four strategic initiatives were engaged: (a) forcibly seize the region from the indigenous people; (b) manufacture a labor force; (c) implement a capitalistic structure that develops the center, while suppressing the periphery in underdevelopment; and (d) secure an economic position of dependency to perpetually fuel the economic enterprise. From a historical perspective, these strategies have resulted in growth in the imperialistic nations, while underdeveloping the nations of the Caribbean.

Noting that structural economists view the world economy as a single unit, not a collage of individual units as with the Caribbean, there is a prevailing acceptance for the economic model that seeks *development* through a concurrent experience of *underdevelopment* (Chilcote, 1984). Tragically, the position ignores the reality of socioeconomic hardship in the periphery. Amin (1974) described the *develop to underdevelop* model as "dominance from the outside" (pp. 18–19). Sunkel and Girvan (1973) extended this position by suggesting that *development* and *underdevelopment* were formed within the same strategy of growth, not as distinct functions generated from separate sources. Sunkel and Girvan (1973) defined *development* and *underdevelopment* as a dependent and concurrent process that represented "the two faces on the historical evolution of the capitalist system" (p. 20). Per the positions of Sunkel and Amin, in order for one culture to develop and flourish, another culture has to suffer through the hardship of underdevelopment. Thus, the realities of external control, intimidating power, development, and underdevelopment are initiated on the intentional exploitation of one society by another (Chilcote, 1984), a situation that has become the foundation of Caribbean life for over five centuries.

Based on the analyzed positions, external control, intimidating power–development, and underdevelopment are not random realities in the Caribbean. Since the stated outcomes for each of the positions include exploitation and underdevelopment, the cultures of the Caribbean have been intentionally confined to a status of *standstill*. The outcomes of this lens are congruent with my observations as a participant.

Theoretical lens II: dependence embedded with chaos—cultural conditioning theory

> Economic dependence is seen as the dominant function and feature of the structure of Caribbean economies.
>
> (Girvan & Girvan, 1973, p. 4)

> One of the more striking features of West Indian development is, that the progress made towards political independence has not been accompanied by parallel advances in the economic field. West Indian territories are still regarded as outstanding examples of dependent economies.
>
> (McIntyre, 1964, p. 165)

Nearly six decades after the African cultures of the Caribbean formed governments and signed emancipation declarations, the island nations remain steeped in first world dependence (Girvan, 2012). Thus, a question that continues to stir anger throughout the region remains unanswered, "Why do we remain underdeveloped and dependent?" In this lens, I will introduce intentional strategies of exploitation that have solidified dependence and generated a violent response from the cultures in the Caribbean.

Identifying chaos

This lens was selected in response to my observations of crisis and chaos in the Caribbean—why is the most gentle, peaceful, loving culture I know besieged with crime and acts of brutality? It is well documented that the Caribbean has the highest crime rate of any region in the world (Table 4.1). Yet, thirty million tourists a year visit the Caribbean due to the graciousness and hospitality of the Afro-Carib culture.[6] There is a something incongruent about those realities—murder, rape, and violent crime are incongruent with loving, giving, gracious, and hospitable. My intimate observations as a resident for nearly two decades suggest that the positive attributes of the culture are authentic, not just a façade manufactured for personal profit. I acknowledge that crime exists in every nation; however, the distinction of the highest murder rate, more police killed per capita, and highest crime rates of any region in the world are not anomalies, they are generated by a debilitating source (Turner, 2014; Table 4.1). This lens seeks to define the source.

As a first hand observer of the confounding phenomenon of crime, in the same day I was held at gunpoint by a group of thieves on the road adjacent to the Rio Cobre River, Jamaica, then robbed by a ten-year-old boy at knifepoint in Spanish Town, Jamaica (Magnified Moment #1). I watched people pillage the car of a man who had just suffered a fatal crash (Magnified Moment #5). Yet, the Afro-Carib culture loved me beyond my definition of love, gave to me when they had little to give, and treated me like I was their own. Thus, the phenomenon of crime in the Caribbean must be analyzed to identify, "Why is this happening?"

Table 4.1 The process of 500 years of chaos in the Caribbean

Chaos	Event	Source
Origin of chaos in the Caribbean	Arrival of Columbus, the rise of imperialism	Columbus & Tosconelli, 2010
Murder	"Taíno leaders burned alive."	Higman, 2011, p. 65
Maiming	Hands of indigenous boys cut off for a lack of production—Method of productivity	Sale, 1991
Biological warfare	Disease utilized as a weapon.	Taylor, 2002
Slaughter	"The great dying."	Wolf, 2010, p. 133
Genocide	Taínos, Arawaks, and Caribs	Higman, 2011, p. 77
Hate	Jews evicted from the Caribbean and declared enemies	Code Noir
Slavery	"Transplanting of people for a profit."	Palmie & Francisco, 2011, p. 132
Barbary	Horrific suffering through the Transatlantic slave trade	Davis, 1997
Revolt	Slave revolts throughout the region	Meeks, 2000
Savagery	Dogs unleashed to hunt and kill slaves	Girard, 2010
Suicide	Mass suicides of slaves on St. John and other islands	Proenza-Coles, 2006
Survival	Resistance battles	Einhorn, 2006
Brutality	Rape, pilfering, and stealing by pirates	Boot, 2002
War	Nazi U-boats and submarines to wage war on trade in the Caribbean	Kelshall, 1988
Assassinations	Political assassinations	Payne, 1994
Crime	Highest homicides rate in world	UNODC, 2014
Corruption	Pervasive government corruption	Transparency International, 2014
Disaster	Natural disasters: hurricanes, floods, earthquakes, and drought	Collymore, 2011
Terrorism	Passenger plane detonated with bomb	Bardach, 2002
Socioeconomic	Perpetual socioeconomic crisis	Girvan, 2007

Cultural conditioning theory

> The most serious blow suffered by the Africans was being removed from history and from the community. Colonization usurps any free role in either war or peace, every decision contributing to his destiny and that of the world, and all cultural and social responsibility.
>
> (Memmi, 1956, p. 91)

E. B. Tylor (1871) defined culture as, "the complex whole which includes knowledge, belief, art, morals, law, customs, and many other capabilities and habits acquired by members of society." Acknowledging that each of the components that define culture are *acquired*, it seems plausible to suggest that individual traits, perspectives, and patterns of behavior could be altered through a culture of control. Memmi (1956), a victim of French colonization in Tunisia, suggests that colonial objectives were satisfied through a culture of violent control. In order to manufacture such a culture required a strategic extraction of growth and potential from the colonized subjects. Thus, the imperialistic colonizers conditioned their enslaved subjects to a single mode of existence—a work force for profit

As the author and director of the Jamaican documentary, *Black Rebels: African Caribbean Freedom Fighters in Jamaica*, Zips (2009) suggested, "the avenue of social self-realization and means of expression in the Caribbean were buried by periods of total control" (p. 43). This reality demands a question, why would the imperialistic colonizers utilize *control* to bury social self-realization and means of expression in the Afro-Carib culture? Memmi (1956), Zips (2009), and Olwig (1985) all suggest that profit was the ultimate motivation to cultural conditioning.

Cultural conditioning: a strategic act to dehumanize

The governance model of *total control* utilized by the imperialistic nations extended beyond modes of expression; *cultural conditioning* was their strategic method to dehumanize the oppressed. Memmi (1956) further suggests that the Africans were only needed for their muscles, which required the European oppressors to dehumanize their enslaved work force in order to achieve what they perceived to be the highest levels of productivity (p. 80). Olwig (1985) took a similar position by stating that the Africans in the Caribbean were reduced to a "status of plantation stock" (p. 93). Both positions imply a strategic intent to dehumanize the culture in order to achieve outcomes of productivity.[7]

Observing the outcomes of cultural conditioning

Striving to adapt to an existence free of imperialistic *control*, the Africans in the Caribbean have struggled to *unbury* modes of *expression and means of self-realization*. However, is it realistic to assume that 500 years of cultural conditioning can be completely *unburied* in sixty years? It seems reasonable to conclude that the process of *unburying* the culture's identity has contributed to political inexperience and errant decisions, which seem to be a factor in the socioeconomic crisis. To hold the African cultures of Caribbean solely responsible for their long-term socioeconomic crisis fails to account for the grueling process required to disengage from 500 years of *cultural conditioning*.

Noting that *cultural conditioning* is a form of intentional dominance seeking an outcome of utter dependence—should expressions of anger or violence be expected from those being dominated? Tierney (1999) suggests that anger should not only be expected, but is justifiable.

> Anger is a justifiable reaction to oppression and is a common experience among disfranchised persons. The failure to recognize the anger of disfranchised groups in the content of oppressive societal conditions has serious ramifications.
>
> (p. 89)

Glickman and Harvey (2013) suggests that the anger within oppressed people can be extreme, which validates my observations as a nearly twenty-year resident in the region.

> Angry people are often not reasonable, and when oppressed people discover their oppression, their response can be more extreme than the cool, detached, and balanced therapist would advise. Yet part of the liberation of minority people must involve discovery of their oppression and the expression of their anger.
>
> (p. 50)

Based on the positions in this segment, me being held at gunpoint and robbed at knifepoint in a culture that has suffered through long-term oppression should not be a surprise.[8] When a culture has observed for 500 years that profit is the result of violent exploitation, shouldn't it be expected that some members of the respective culture do as they were taught? Further, when a culture has been collectively disrespected and conditioned not to use their intellect or creative capacity to innovate, how should members of the culture be expected to respond to dominating dependency? Shouldn't it be expected that members will respond to dominating dependency as they were conditioned?

In the light of these positions, the reality of emancipated independence is based on a false assumption that suggests that a signature on a declaration instantly equates to a holistic independence. *Cultural conditioning* was a strategic act that continues to fortify long-term dependence for the African cultures in the Caribbean. Therefore, it seems plausible to suggest that sustainable growth for the Caribbean cultures is contingent on the restoration of social self-realization and means of expression.

Chaos theory: the initial conditions in the origin are relevant

> Chaos is a science of process rather than a state, a becoming rather than a beginning.
>
> (Gleick, 1987, p. 5)

Chaos is a process of becoming, not a random reality of confusion, disorder, and uncertainty (Gleick, 1987). Further, the process of chaos does not possess properties of randomness, but is an outcome of the initial conditions in the past (Capra & Luisi, 2014; Runco, 2014). An anonymous truism seems to appropriately describe the reality of chaos—*We know a lot about our future based on our past* (as cited in Capra, 2002). Applying the same lens to the African cultures of the Caribbean, the socioeconomic chaos in the present is a reflection of the initial conditions in the past. In contrast, an analysis of the socioeconomic realities in the initial conditions illuminate hope for cultural restoration in the present and future (Capra & Luisi, 2014). This theoretical section magnifies the effect of chaos on the current, present, and future socioeconomic conditions in the Caribbean.

Initial conditions in the Caribbean

Chaos is a prevailing theme interwoven throughout each of the historical eras of the Caribbean (Table 4.1). Beginning in the decolonization era, political powers aggressively sought to ease the level of chaos; however, the current state of socioeconomic chaos in the region suggests that the attempts were unsuccessful (Girvan, 2011). Capra suggests that any solution designed to diffuse chaos in its current state is futile—a Band-Aid on a viral infection is not a sustainable response (2002). He further argues that a state of chaos can be transformed into a process of life and growth if the solutions are specifically developed to address the initial conditions in the past, not the present reality (Capra, 2002). Thus, healthy paths for the future are contingent on identifying and rectifying dysfunctional factors in the origin of a living organism.

Although the quantity and depth of the *process* of chaos in the Caribbean expands well beyond the list in Table 4.1, the dysfunctional atrocities are the foundational blocks on which the region is rooted.

As noted in Table 4.1, the *process of becoming* for the Africans in the Caribbean has been saturated in dysfunctional chaos. Césaire (1950) referenced the process when he wrote, "The Africans of the Caribbean suffer in the flesh from all the wrong doings of history, from all the universal wrongs" (p. 78). Naipaul (1969) suggested "the events of the overwhelming past," would keep the Caribbean from ever achieving a respectable position (p. 29). Thus, it seems plausible to suggest that the dominant factor in today's chaos in the Caribbean is found in the initial conditions on which the region was established. The credibility of the claim and hope of a sustainable future for the Afro-Caribs is established in a deeper analysis of the chaos theory that follows.

Order beneath chaos

When nineteenth century mathematician Poincaré published his theories on non-linear dynamics, he recognized he was "gazing at the footprint of chaos" (as cited in Stewart, 2002, p. 72). However, due to Einstein's theory of relativity and Planck's theories of energy quanta, Poincaré's mathematics of visual imagery went unnoticed for eight decades (Capra, 2014). Through a theory he called Topology, Poincaré argued that traditional geometrical shapes and concepts such as a triangle, line, or area could be "distorted at will" (as cited in Capra, 2014, p. 107). Further, he suggested that his topology was a "mathematics of relationships, of unchangeable, or invariant patterns" (as cited in Stewart, 2002, p. 71; Capra, 2014, p. 108). Based on Poincaré's topological method, researchers can now "solve non-linear equations associated with chaotic phenomena and discover order beneath the seeming chaos" (Capra, 2014, p. 109).

The socioeconomic chaos in the Caribbean is a non-linear, complex problem that has yet to be solved. The problem in its current state of chaos is defined by erratic and complex patterns of socioeconomic crisis. The chaotic patterns strongly suggest disorder; yet, when the problem is analyzed through the lens of chaos theory, there is an origin of order beneath the chaos that defines the state of becoming.

The origin of order in the Caribbean is the intentional *distortion* of culture in the initial conditions of the region. When the peaceful region and its cultures were violently *distorted at will* to secure a profit, the *distortion* prohibited cultural growth and generated a dysfunctional progression that intensified chaos with each generation. Due to the scope and scale of the chaos, there seems to be no solution to the disorder. However, an analysis of the *distortion* in the initial conditions is not limited to "why" there is chaos in the Caribbean, it also identifies "what" and "how" must be implemented to dismantle chaos and restore sustainable socioeconomic growth.

"Why" the distortion in the initial conditions matter

Poincaré's breakthrough removed the erratic and random attributes of chaos and opened the door for other scientists to solve non-linear phenomenon through patterns of relationship. One of those scientists was meteorologist Edward Lorenz, who developed patterns of weather by using Poincaré's method for solving non-linear equations. Lorenz (1972) suggested that monumental consequences were the result of small changes in an initial state of being (Capra, 2014). The analogy associated with his theoretical position is termed "the butterfly effect" (Runco, 2014, p. 83). Although Lorenz's full description of the butterfly effect is steeped in jest, it states that an extensive storm in New York could be caused by a disturbance from a butterfly flying in Beijing (as cited in Capra, 2014). Runco (2014) references the analogy when he defines chaos as, "sensitive dependence on initial conditions"

(p. 407). In the context of this project, Chaos Theory answers an elusive question for the Africans in the Caribbean—"Why is this happening to us?" The *initial conditions* in the formative years of the Caribbean are a catalyst of elevated chaos in the present.

The initial conditions are currently relevant

For the Africans in Caribbean, three patterns of relationship appear critical: (1) disorder has become a pattern of order; (2) the randomness of hardship has meaning; and (3) crisis has process.[9] Each of those patterns seem dysfunctional; however, chaos theory, which functions independently from scale, has been used in a wide range of disciplines to explain and solve irregularities (Runco, 2014). The irregularities that explain proteins, lighting, stars, blood vessels, electrical circuitry, and economies, are a few significant explanations that stem from within chaos theory (Runco, 2014). In the context of the Caribbean, the disorders of dehumanization, egregious violence, and cultural conditioning are irregularities that provide *meaning* and explanation to the chaos in the present.

Utilizing the irregularities in the initial conditions to illuminate meaning, this project answers three questions of inquiry

(1) What essential cultural expressions or components were extracted from the culture in the initial conditions?
(2) Does the absence of any of the expressions or components provide meaning to the current socioeconomic chaos in the Caribbean?
(3) If cultural expressions or essential components were restored back into the culture, what meaning would be provided?

The answers to each of these questions are expanded in Chapters 3, 4, and 6.

Extracted, absent, and restored

Examples of extracted and absent components in the *initial conditions* in the Caribbean are self-realization, creative practice, and innovation. Acknowledging that all living systems require conscious creativity to generate and regenerate (Capra: 2014, p. xi; Runco: 2014, p. 352), the absence of creativity in the *initial conditions* has produced a chaotic effect in the present—a state of becoming. According to Runco (2014), the absence of creative practice in a culture or individual removes a sense of self, place, and realized potential—each provide self-realization and meaningful expressions of cultural value. Noting that the imperialistic agenda included a suppression of cognitive processes that included creative practice, imagination, and the art of civilization (Olwig, 1985; Zips, 2009), the absence extracted the true cultural identity and facilitated socioeconomic outcomes of chaos (Runco, 2014). However, the meaning provided from the extracted and absent components identifies the origin of restoration for the Caribbean cultures. The meaning extracted suggests that the origin to restoration for the cultures in the Caribbean is an intentional implementation of creative practice.[10]

Summation of chaos theory

The intentional acts of imperialistic greed and oppression in 1492 set in motion a chaotic socioeconomic storm that negatively affects the everyday lives of nearly forty million people in the Caribbean. The positions of Girvan, Gleick, Capra, Runco, Poincaré, and Lorenz, establish chaos theory as a relevant explanation on why the Africans in the Caribbean remain in socioeconomic crisis. The *presence* of debilitating acts and the *absence* of essential cultural expression in

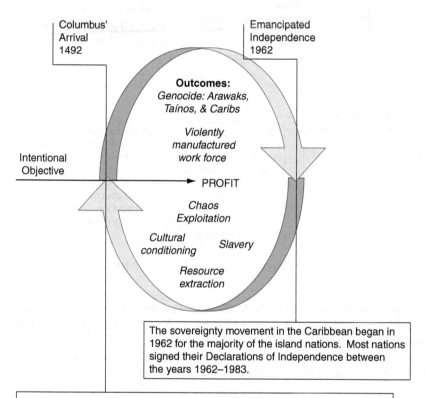

Figure 4.1 The intentional socioeconomic history of the Caribbean: 1492–1962.

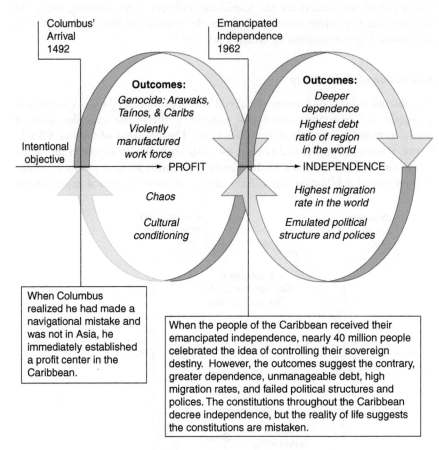

Figure 4.2 The intentional socioeconomic history of the Caribbean: 1962–present.

the initial conditions have methodically increased the intensity of chaos and created an atmosphere of despair, which has facilitated a dependency on first world nations (Girvan, 2011). Through the lens of chaos theory, the Caribbean's socioeconomic crisis has a meaningful pattern of order, which in turn has identified a path of creative practice for sustainable growth.

Theoretical lens III: strength through restoration— intentional creative practice

> The history of the islands can never be satisfactorily told. History is built around achievement and creation; and nothing was created in the West Indies.
>
> (Naipaul (1969, p. 29), a Trinidadian born Nobel Prize recipient in Literature)

As the Caribbean struggles to find new ways to generate growth and greater consideration, there is a strong case for reorienting our thinking.

(Jessop (2014, p. 1), the Director of the Caribbean Council)

Socioeconomic projections regarding the future of the Caribbean suggest that crisis will continue to escalate.[11] The Royal Bank of the Caribbean (Royal Caribbean Bank, 2016), The International Monetary Fund (2015), and The World Bank (World Bank Group, 2015) all project similar socioeconomic outcomes for the region. Based on the findings in this project, the question of "why" long-term socioeconomic crisis continues to inhibit the Caribbean has been answered—the initial conditions, strategies of cultural conditioning, dependency, underdevelopment, migration, and unrealized potential are all explanations for the socioeconomic crisis. Therefore, the next step in the progression of inquiry is developed around a future of sustainable growth for the Caribbean—"Where is the door of hope for the cultures in the Caribbean?"

Augusto de le Torre (2013) and David Jessop (2014)—Regional Chief Economists for the World Bank and Director of the Caribbean Council respectively—suggest there is a clearly defined door of hope for the region. Although the door is aggressively closing, an intentional decision to embrace the reality on the other side of the door is required to assimilate into a growth mode—"As the economic tailwinds continue to die, growth has to come from within, and innovation and dynamism are the key if the region is going to grow" (de la Torre, p. 1). This project has identified the intentional implementation of creative practice as a door of *growth from within*, a path that should ease hardship and produce *innovation and dynamism* for the Caribbean cultures (Figure 4.3).

Noting that the tenets of "socioeconomic growth do not lose their application in times of crisis," an essential tenet of sustainable growth is active environments of creative practice (Bilchitz, 2013, p. 1). Runco (2014) further argues that sustainable growth is contingent on the access to environments of creative practice. Referencing the Africans in the Caribbean, Naipaul (1969), Memmi (1956), Olwig (1985), and Rodney (1972) suggests that creative practice was strategically suppressed to secure underdevelopment in the Caribbean. The strategic suppression resulted in non-sustainable development and long-term socioeconomic crisis—a state of becoming that produced chaotic disorder. Thus, the third theoretical lens stands in direct contrast to the reprehensible strategies of the imperialistic oppressors, which was a cultural conditioning with an objective of cultural suppression. This lens will argue that the intentional implementation of creative practice will result in cultural restoration and socioeconomic freedom.[12]

Acknowledging that a cultural restoration requires a *re-orienting of thinking*, this theoretical lens addresses the nuances, benefits, and potential outcomes of implementing creative practice as a method for easing socioeconomic crisis in the Caribbean. Further, through this lens I will argue that intentional and active creative practice is a path to independence, a solution to long-term hardship, and a reality for sustainable growth for the Africans in the Caribbean.

Creative practice: the internal dynamic

Well intentioned political leaders have developed policies and structures in an effort to eradicate long-term socioeconomic crisis in the region. However, dependency and crisis remain inhibitors of achievement and growth for the Africans in the Caribbean (Girvan, 2011). Seeking a path to autonomy, this project seeks to illuminate a missing component within the implemented policies and structures. Brewster (1971) suggests that the absence of a vital component within socioeconomic structure results in dysfunction.

> Economic dependence may be defined as a lack of capacity to manipulate the operative elements of an economic system. Such a situation is characterized by an absence of inter-dependence between the economic functions of a system. This lack of inter-dependence implies that the system has no internal dynamic, which could enable it to function as independent, autonomous, entity.
>
> (Brewster, 1971, p. 1)

Socioeconomic health of a region is contingent on an *internal dynamic* that facilitates independence and autonomy; Runco (2014), Capra (2014), and Rodney (1972) suggest that the *internal dynamic* is intentional and active environments of creative practice. Further, when addressing the socioeconomic components of development, resilience, productivity, and independence; active creative practice is an essential *internal dynamic* for sustainable growth (Runco, 2014).[13]

However, creative practice as a key component of political reform or social change has been historically marginalized. Runco (2014) suggests "political conditions influence the expression of creativity and the fulfillment of creative potential" (p. 303). Based on the stated positions, the marginalization of creative practice in political policy has diffused the *internal dynamic* that facilitates independence and autonomy. Regarding the cultures of the Caribbean, the path out of socioeconomic chaos (Figure 4.3) requires political leaders to intentionally guide creative practice to the center of national policy to achieve a sustainable future.[14]

Intentional cultural restoration

The structural components of *cultural restoration* in the Caribbean must be formed to satisfy two objectives: (1) dismantle the effects of cultural conditioning by unburying modes of cultural expression; and (2) provide a clear and realistic path for sustainable growth. *Unburying* cultural expressions requires an intentional rehabilitation of cultural components that have been strategically suppressed for more than 500 years. Through cultural conditioning, imperialistic nations strategically coerced the Africans in the Caribbean to refrain from cultivating sustainable attributes like creativity, imagination,

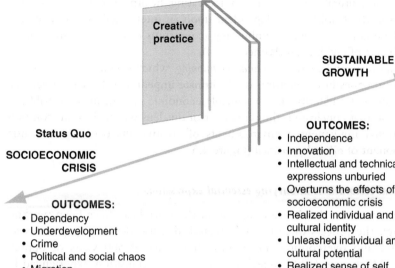

Creative practice

SUSTAINABLE GROWTH

Status Quo

SOCIOECONOMIC CRISIS

OUTCOMES:
- Dependency
- Underdevelopment
- Crime
- Political and social chaos
- Migration
- Educational insufficiencies
- Unrealized potential
- Unrecognized sense of self
- Unstable sense of place
- High debt ratio
- Exploitation
- Resource deficit
- Stagnate or digressing economy
- Unstable social structures

OUTCOMES:
- Independence
- Innovation
- Intellectual and technical expressions unburied
- Overturns the effects of socioeconomic crisis
- Realized individual and cultural identity
- Unleashed individual and cultural potential
- Realized sense of self
- Embeds essential attributes of sustainable growth
- Ensured survival
- Self-regulating environment
- Produces development
- Stimulates healthy change
- Healthy socioeconomic outcomes
- Source of resilience
- Productive future
- Elevates the whole
- A gauge of stability
- Solutions of a cultural value

Figure 4.3 The door of HOPE for the Caribbean.

and the art of civilization.[15] Conditioning the culture to illiteracy and depriving it of cognitive attributes impeded its ability to create a stable socioeconomic foundation at its emancipation. Blouet (1990) expanded on this idea when she stated, "Education might provide the surest foundation for the creation of a stable socio-economic framework" (p. 126). This tragic reality in the Caribbean is reflected in Kant's philosophical position: "The external power that deprives man of the freedom to communicate his thoughts publicly deprives him at the same time of his freedom to think" (as cited in Scott, 1990, p. 118). An example of an intentional act to suppress cultural expression is the 1797 law in Barbados that made it illegal to teach African slaves to read or write (The Library of Congress, 1987). According to Rodney (1972), "those whom colonists could not readily exploit were not offered even the crumbs of education" (p. 240). Thus, dismantling the effects of cultural conditioning and creating healthy socioeconomic outcomes in the Caribbean is dependent upon an intentional grassroots educational initiative focused on unburying expressions of creativity, innovation, and the art of civilization (Runco, 2014).

Long-term and strategic *cultural conditioning*, which sought to suppress cognitive processes in the culture, is a legitimate impediment for true independence, authentic identity, and sustainable economic growth in the Caribbean. Based on that conclusion, the remainder of this lens will analyze outcomes of intentional implemented environments of creative practice as an essential component of *cultural restoration* (Figure 4.3).

Cultural restoration: unburying essential expressions

Since the 1960s, the African cultures of the Caribbean have been working through the process of losing a legislated identity, developing policies for growth, and overcoming the emotional trauma of 500 years of oppression.[16] Mackenzie (1990) references the difficult transition experienced by colonies moving from an imperialistic to decolonized model, "the transition involves more than a set of economic, political, and military phenomenon, it is also a complex ideology which has widespread cultural, intellectual, and technical expressions" (p. 78). Therefore, due to *cultural conditioning* in the colonized era and the reality of long-term socioeconomic crisis, it seems plausible to suggest that the potential of intellectual and technical expressions remain buried. Socio-culturist Miguel Zavala (2013) has defined the process of *unburying* cultural expressions as "an anti-colonial struggle that grows out of grassroots spaces" (p. 55). To unbury the expressions, which counter the damaging consequences of long-term *cultural conditioning* and sever the ties to first world dependency, it is imperative that an intentional grassroots *restoration* strategy be implemented. An intentional grassroots strategy develops and facilitates environments that intentionally unbury authentic intellectual and technical expressions—a framework that is configured around authentic design.

The Harvard Family Research Project developed an example of a grassroots design framework (Caspe, 2010). The initiative forms environments that promote innovation through a "design thinking framework" (Caspe, 2010, p. 1). The project utilizes an implementation approach developed by an innovation and design firm named IDEO.[17] The approach utilizes "three overlapping 'spaces' that allow for innovation to emerge: inspiration, ideation, and implementation" (Caspe, 2010). For the cultures of the Caribbean to unbury authentic technical and intellectual expressions requires access to environments that allow students to understand problems and opportunities, space to brainstorm and test ideas, and the freedom to implement their respective ideas (Caspe, 2010).

Unburying cultural expression: transforming place, potential, and self

Establishing active environments of creative practice embeds health into three essential social components—*place, potential,* and *self* (Runco, 2014). *Place* is a collective identity, *potential* is stifled or unleashed, and *self* is shaped through a cultural environment. The transformation of *place, potential,* and *self* has the potential to dismantle the effects of socioeconomic crisis throughout the culture (Rodney, 1972).[18]

Place is a collective identity—if the collective reality of "home" is developed through oppression, violence, or crisis, then the collective identity becomes a barrier to growth since life is filtered through those attributes. In contrast, if the collective reality of "home" is developed through the progression of active creative practice, innovation, and accomplishment, then the collective identity becomes a realized environment of courage and aspiration.[19]

The struggle for true identity for the African's in the Caribbean is reflected in Walcott's play, *Dream on Monkey Mountain* (Walcott, 1970). The play tells a story about an African in the Caribbean named Makak, who is approaching the end of his life and determined to understand his true identity. Makak recognizes that when he speaks English he reflects his European conditioning, yet, when he adheres to cultural traditions rooted in Africa, he is "repeating the authoritative claim of the colonizer as the superiority of their culture and language" (as Sinnewe, p. 116). When Makak settles on the vernacular of English established from centuries of slavery, he concedes to the duel identity rooted in Europe and Africa.[20]

As a nearly two-decade resident of the Caribbean, I have witnessed the Afro-Carib struggle to realize their true identity due to their collective perspective of *place*. The long-term struggle has allowed perspectives of crime, poverty, drugs, corruptness, and idleness to tragically become a global identity for the culture. However, based on two decades of observations, the perspectives are not aligned with the values or positions that the African cultures of the Caribbean reflect.

In this project, I am seeking to establish a path of true identity, one that reflects the uniqueness of the culture, while facilitating independence and development. To effectively develop the path this project will answer a critical question—"How can the Africans of the Caribbean move beyond the false identities and establish a true identity?" Answering the question begins by analyzing the unrealized *potential* of the culture beyond crisis, recognizing the value of *place*, and identifying an essential lens of understanding. Each of three components facilitates action beyond the escalating crisis.

Unburying cultural expression: transforming identity by unleashing potential

The value of unleashed potential has yet to be realized for the Africans in the Caribbean. Eric Williams, Trinidad and Tobago's first Prime Minister proposed, "The entire Caribbean Basin could hold a dignified global position if the African culture would realize its potential" (1993, p. 148). Based on the historical record and the present reality of crisis, Grugel (1995) suggests that the long term socioeconomic crisis in the Caribbean prevents the culture from realizing their potential. He argues,

> A series of crises in the Caribbean prevents the people of the region from realizing their potential. Unless these problems are addressed, the region will continue to face deepening poverty for most of the population, *whatever* the macroeconomic situation, and thus potential political instability.
>
> (p. 233)

Due to the length and weight of the socioeconomic crisis, the culture has seemingly surrendered its potential for authentic innovation, which reduces life to daily decisions of survival. Recognizing the need to transform their identity, Shepherd (2011) suggested that an awakened consciousness and purpose for the Africans in the Caribbean would only come through realized *potential*. Grugel (1995), Williams (1993), and Shepherd (2011) have all suggested that regardless of the political or economic structures, crisis will continue to abound unless individuals can move past a survivalist mentality and realize their full *potential* for authentic expressions of innovation.

Thus, the reason that political structures and/or economic policies have not proved to be viable solutions to the socioeconomic crisis in the Caribbean is their failure to prioritize the culture's full *potential*. The Africans in the Caribbean cannot move beyond their current status and establish a true identity based solely on political structures or economic policies. When Runco (2014) spoke of unrealized potential, he also argued, "creating a sense of self" is imperative for independence and sustainable development (p. 219). Based on Runco's (2014) position, true identity and realized potential are both products of a sense of self.

Unburying cultural expression: realized sense of self

Both Richard Florida (2002) and Mark Runco (2014), a socioeconomic theorist and one of the foremost scholars of multi-disciplinary creativity, respectively, have argued that it's essential for individuals to establish a "sense of self" in order for a human culture to grow and develop (Runco, 2014, p. 219). Florida (2002) wrote;

> Where people once found themselves bound together by social institutions and formed by their identities in groups, a fundamental characteristic today is that we strive to create our own identities. It is this creation and re-creation of the self, often in ways that reflect our creativity, that is the key feature of a creative effort. In this new world, it is no longer the organization we work for, churches, neighborhoods, or even family ties

that define us. Instead, we do this ourselves, defining our identity along the dimensions of our creativity.

(p. 7)

When the Africans were violently removed from their homelands and placed in the Caribbean, they were intentionally detached from their *sense of self*. Their freedom to *strive for their own identities* was removed and reconstituted by imperialistic legislation and enslavement—their *sense of self* was shaped by the horrific conditions that defined their reality of life. Memmi (1956) further explained this detachment; "The Africans were removed from history and from the community, which usurps any free role in either war or peace, every decision contributing to their destiny and that of the world, and all cultural and social responsibility" (p. 91).

Further deteriorating a *sense of self*, while the imperialistic nations strategically displaced Africans in the Caribbean, they were concurrently dehumanizing and conditioning the culture to refrain from using their minds, engaging in creative practice, and producing anything of individualized value. Thus, it seems logical to conclude that a *sense of self* for the Africans in the Caribbean has been intentionally stripped away by the convergence of two inhumane experiences, a violent displacement from their homelands and the intentional suppression of creative practice.[21]

Forfeiting a *sense of self* is a surrendering of creative practice (Florida, 2002)—innovation is the outcome of creative practice. In contrast, a realized *sense of self* produces individual growth and cultural innovation that weakens an atmosphere of dependency. Based on the positions of Runco (2014), Florida (2002), and Grugel (1995), a realized *sense of self* stimulates creative practice, which shapes identity and facilitates independence. Therefore, the intentional suppression of creative practice seems to rob the collective culture of a *sense of self* and opportunity, which is a central source of socioeconomic crisis in the Caribbean.

Unburying cultural expressions and strategically moving beyond the current position of socioeconomic hardship requires an intentional cultural restoration through active environments of creative practice. A 2012 Adobe research project on creative practice revealed,

> eight out of ten people feel that unlocking creativity is critical to economic growth and nearly two-thirds of the respondents feel creativity is valuable to society, yet a striking minority—only one in four people believe they are living up to their own creative potential.
>
> (Naiman, 2014, www.creativityatwork.com)

Negus and Pickering (2004) argued,

> Creativity is continually regarded as the source of challenge to rules and conventions, as a way of recombining different aspects of tradition and

knowledge in their previous arrangements, and perhaps most importantly, as a means to move beyond existing horizons of experience.

(p. 9)

Since a transformation of identity, sense of self, cultural growth, and independence are dependent on active environments of creative practice, the Africans in the Caribbean have an opportunity to modify their cultural DNA, *move beyond their existing horizons of experience*, and unbury authentic cultural expressions through the strategic facilitation of creative practice.

Essential attributes of sustainable growth: create and re-generate

From a molecular position, sustainable growth for every living organism is contingent on two essential attributes, the capacity to create and regenerate (Capra, 2014). Fritjof Capra and Pier Luisi (2014)—two scholars who work in a number of different fields, including physics, systems theory, chemistry, and natural science—have suggested that sustainable growth in all living networks is exclusively dependent on self-generation. Living networks must perpetually *create or recreate* themselves by transforming or replacing dysfunctional elements that threaten their existence. If the capacity to *create or re-create* is suppressed or denied, then the living organism becomes unstable, dysfunctional, and ultimately "dies in isolation" (Capra & Luisi, 2014, p. 130).[22] Capra and Luisi further argue that when dying organisms are intentionally implanted with the capacities to *create or regenerate*, their trajectory of existence is altered from death to life (2014).

Acknowledging that the African culture in the Caribbean is defined as a *living organism*, the socioeconomic conditions in the region suggest that cultural death is an imminent reality based on Capra and Luisi's model (2014). The strategic suppression of the *create and recreate* capacities with outcomes of long-term instability and debilitating crisis are indicators that the region is on a trajectory of isolated death. Thus, the region is challenged with a decision of urgency, continue on a trajectory of death by remaining status quo, or restore life and sustainable growth through environments that facilitate the life giving attributes of *create and recreate*.[23] The remaining content of this lens will utilize established positions to illuminate outcomes of intentionally implemented environments of creative practice.

Intentional environments of creative practice produce sustainable growth

Runco (2014), a cognitive psychologist and foremost scholar of multi-disciplinary creativity, defined and identified outcomes of creativity.

In a phrase, creativity is a vital form of human capital. Creativity both contributes to the information explosion and helps us cope and adapt to the resulting challenges.

(p. xi)

Parsing Runco's position, significant challenges such as socioeconomic crisis require coping and adaptive mechanisms—the former to insure survival, the latter to secure sustainable growth. Therefore, facilitating environments of creative practice ensures that the culture will cope with change and adapt to growth. Due to the challenges and necessity of change, a constant flow of creativity enables a living system to meet the demands of internal and peripheral flux (Capra & Luisi, 2014). Contrastingly, the culture that suppresses open access to environments of creative practice forfeits its coping mechanisms, has limited capacity to adapt to growth, and enables cultural chaos.

As a form of human capital, creativity is an essential asset for every nation, culture, and community that seeks sustainable growth. However, as Runco (2014) has argued, "creativity is partly intentional, partly a matter of choice" (p. 419). For the cultures of the Caribbean, intentional access to creative practice determines the value of its people, which is its most precious and essential asset. Suppressed access devalues the people, limits choice, and denies growth. Open access to creative practice increases the value of the people, reinforces self-realization, and enables sustainable growth, all of which dismantle the justification for migration. Runco (2014), Capra and Luisi (2014), and Torrance (Millar, 1995) all argued that creativity is essential for a living system to survive, grow, and flourish beyond the challenges of existence.

Intentional environments of creative practice ensure survival

A decision to integrate creative practice into the highest level of policy and process requires, "a courageous decision" (Runco, 2014, p. 319). Paul Torrance, a psychologist, renowned scholar of creativity, and founder of the "Future Problem Solving Program International," was asked to design a survival program for the United States Air Force (as cited in Runco, 2014, p. 319; Millar, 1995). Seeking to increase the probability of survival in an intense and chaotic environment, Torrance identified seven key characteristics that elevated the probability for a sustainable life. The characteristics he identified were: "inventiveness, creativity, imagination, originality, flexibility, courage, and decision-making skills" (as cited in Runco, 2014, p. 319). As Torrance conducted the research, "he learned that the underlying element of survival is creativity, which is essential for producing constructive behavior and unusual achievements" (Hebert, Cramond, Speirs, Millar, & Silvian, 2002, p. 7). Although all of Torrance's sustainable life characteristics are directly correlated with survival in an *intense and chaotic* environment, it should be noted that the choice to implement environments of creative practice prompts a consideration for life beyond a mode of survival (Runco, 2014). From the survival experiences, Torrance developed what he called his non-academic definition of survival creativity, "Whenever one is faced with a problem for which he has no practiced or learned solution, creativity is required" (Millar, 1995, p. 39). Noting that fear is a factor associated with situations which no prior knowledge or expertise exists, courage is required to engage creativity, which illuminates a path out of the problem. Further, in the context of the Caribbean's *intense and chaotic* environment, a courageous decision to intentionally implement environments of creative practice in response to socioeconomic crisis could produce *constructive behavior and unique achievements*.

Suppressed environments of creative practice produce underdevelopment

Walter Rodney (1972), a Guyanese sociologist, expanded on the essential components required for a culture to move beyond underdevelopment; those components are—"increased skill and capacity, greater freedom, creativity, self-discipline, responsibility, and material wellbeing" (p. 9). Noting that the suppression of individualized creativity, through the strategic act of dehumanization, forfeited or distorted the *capacity, skill, freedom, self-discipline, responsibility, and material well being* in the cultures of the Caribbean, the suppression fortified underdevelopment.

Preparing for his documentary titled, *Black Rebels: African Caribbean Freedom Fighters in Jamaica*, Zips (2009) discovered that the expressions of religion, music, and dance were all prohibited, while drums and instruments of percussion were burned in order to deconstruct any sense of place for the cultures in the Caribbean. Although it could be argued that music, dance, and musical instruments have little impact on development, the suppression prohibited expressions of value and personal growth for the cultures. Rodney (1972) further argued that the difference between developed and underdeveloped is, "the environment in which the human groups evolved" (1972, p. 9). Since the Africans in the Caribbean evolved in an environment in which environments of creative practice were strategically suppressed, underdevelopment became the evolutionary outcome. Thus, in order to deconstruct the current outcome of underdevelopment, the cultures must embrace a development strategy that is stabilized with cultural expressions of value—environments of creative practice that produce innovation and other cultural expressions that secure development.

Intentional environments of creative practice produce healthy socioeconomic outcomes

Active and open access to environments of creative practice is an essential source of adaptive growth for the Caribbean cultures. Gunderson and Holling (2002), scholars of the Panarchy adaptive cycle for complex systems identified a cultural growth lifeline through the phases of an adaptive cycle: "There are phases marked by opportunity, creativity, and novelty—where good things happen" (p. 55). Based on their hypothesis, the *opportunity* for *creativity* results in *novelty* of value. When cultures have the opportunity to embrace free and open environments of creative practice, novelty items of sustainable growth is the outcome. Thus, providing intentional opportunities of creative practice is essential for *good things to happen*. *Good things* in the context of a living culture suggests the resilient presence of strength, productivity, and health.

Contrastingly, the omission or suppression of opportunities to embrace the creativity phase on the adaptive cycle develops a chaotic, dysfunctional outcome, one that prohibits the culture from reaching *good things*. Bryan Norton (2005), a public policy scholar, suggested "creativity" on the Adaptive Cycle for sustainability is the "basis for productivity" (p. 121). Since creative practice is essential to productivity, a living system requires the presence of creativity to achieve healthy outcomes and avoid crisis. Further, if the function of creative practice is suppressed or surrendered to hegemonic nations, it suggests that the opportunity and novelty phases are also controlled by the hegemonic nation, which is an environment of total control. The Panarchy model of adaptive growth illuminates the necessity for the Caribbean cultures to provide opportunities for personal growth through environments of creative practice. The outcomes of novelty and innovative value are sustainable functions that define socioeconomic health, a plausible reality for the forty million people living in the Caribbean.

Intentional environments of creative practice stimulate change

Responding to the economic suppression and dependence in the Caribbean, the Trinidadian economist C. L. R. James (1983) proposed a way to move beyond a system of dependency in the Caribbean: "trust in economic creativity" (p. 154). Accordingly, a culture that fails to trust in the uniqueness of its creative individuality is confined to an incongruent or dependent economic model—both perpetuate a static, dependent plantation system that prohibits freedom and independence. Contrastingly, the reality of independence and freedom requires a courageous decision to trust in the creative individuality of the respective members of a culture (Runco, 2014, p. 319).

Seeking to clarify the outcomes of an intentional decision of *economic creativity*, Runco (2014) claimed,

> Independence, like freedom, seems to be tied to creativity on multiple levels of analysis … it is the disposition towards independence and the capacity to think in an autonomous fashion that leads to ideas and solutions that are different, contrarian, and original.
>
> (p. 310)

Based on the positions of Runco (2014) and James (1983), if the cultures in the Caribbean genuinely desire to move beyond economic models of dependency and attain a transformative change of independence, the culture must intentionally trust in its creative individuality that emanates from environments of creative practice.

Intentional environments of creative practice are a source of resilience

When referencing socioeconomic uncertainty, Thomas Homer-Dixon (2006), a scholar of international governance and innovation, stated, "resilience in the face of constant change demands constant creativity" (p. 161). Homer-Dixon is suggesting that sustainable growth will constantly be challenged by an unrelenting change; however, if cultural leaders remain fixed to familiar paths that devalue the influence of creativity, then constant change will consume the culture. Thus, implementing and honoring the value cultural creativity is a method of resilience that overcomes constant change and establishes socioeconomic certainty. Homer-Dixon furthers states, "possibilities and renewal are a source of immense creativity" (Homer-Dixon, 2006, p. 19). In light of Homer-Dixon's socioeconomic assessment, the longstanding polices and political structures in the Caribbean have produced extended hardship, such that *possibilities and renewal* have been hindered due to the suppression of *immense creativity*. Runco (2014) has stated, "political conditions influence the expression of creativity and the fulfillment of creative potential" (p. 303). In order for *possibilities and renewal* to become a constant source of resilience in the Caribbean, political leadership must have the courage to develop environments that *demand constant creativity*. A political influence that governs to fulfill the creative potential of their respective culture facilitates resilience and provides an environment of *possibilities and renewal*.

Intentional environments of creative practice produce a productive future

Referencing socioeconomic crises and the hope for survival, social justice scholar Francis Moore Lappe (2011) affirmed, the "key to our future is our deep capacity for creativity" (p. 196). The *key* to a healthy productive future for the Caribbean cultures is a courageous decision to intentionally develop a comprehensive initiative to increase the structural capacity for creative practice. However, achieving a productive future according to Lappe (2011), includes an adherence to a *deep capacity* for creativity. Lappe's position suggests that a shallow or weak effort to develop individualized creativity would not generate a productive environment or a sustainable future. Runco (2014) expanded on the cultural significance of *deep capacity* for creativity when he stated, "Any time one creative idea is ignored or dismissed because of the social pressures, it is actually an associative chain of possibilities that is lost" (p. 159). The cultures of the Caribbean have lost over 500 years of possibilities and productiveness due to suppressed creative practice, yet a productive and sustainable future remains a present reality through the development of a free and deep capacity for creative practice within the culture.

Intentional environments of creative practice elevate the whole

Paul Guilford (1950), former president of the American Psychological Association and human behavior scholar, has argued "Creativity is a natural resource and efforts to encourage creativity would pay high dividends to the whole of society" (as cited in Runco, 2014, p. 444). Thus, strategic development of environments of creative practice elevates the whole of the living system. In addition, it should be re-stated that creative practice is, "a vital form of capital" (Runco, 2014, p. xi). Therefore, recognizing that the Caribbean has a population of nearly forty million residents, the region has access to *a vital form of capital* that has the creative potential to elevate the whole of the region. Based on Guilford's (1950) logic, discouraging creative practice or broad dependence on outside forces for innovative advancement are detriments to the whole of the region. The intentional encouragement and implementation of environments of creative practice elevates the whole of the region through culturally derived innovation.

Intentional environments of creative practice are a gauge of stability

A healthy sense of place is directly correlated with the effectiveness and influence of environments of creative practice (Runco, 2014). Memmi (1956), who was raised in a colonized environment in Tunisia and wrote *The Colonizer and the Colonized* has suggested,

> The most serious blow suffered by the Africans was being removed from history and from the community where colonization usurps any free role in either war or peace, every decision contributing to their destiny and that of the world, and all cultural and social responsibility.
>
> (p. 91)

Based on Memmi's (1956) assessment, losing a sense of place for the colonized Africans was defined as an extraction of process, which includes processes of creativity, innovation, and any decision related to sustainable growth. Having their minds intentionally closed to key components of sustainable life, the only realistic identity for the enslaved Africans in the Caribbean was one of cultural demise. Thus, a destabilized sense of place is directly correlated migration, suppression of self-growth, and the absence of environments of creative practice.

Florida (2002) confirms that an environment that encourages creative practice and innovation stimulates a stable sense of place.

> Frustrated by the limits of conventional wisdom and even more how economic development was actually being practiced, I began asking people how they chose where to live and work. My conclusion was that rather than being driven exclusively by companies, economic growth was occurring in places that were tolerant, diverse, and open to creativity.
>
> (As cited in Runco, 2014, p. 352)

Based on Florida's (2002) research, a stable sense of place can be defined by openness to creative practice. Yet, when self-growth through environments of creative practice is absent from a culture, the internal need to create and innovate produces a flight mentality.[24] The International Monetary Fund (2005) determined that the Caribbean has the highest rate of migration of any region in the world; 40% of its labor force has migrated in the last decade. Some island nations "have lost up to 70% of their work force with more than 12 years of schooling, which is the highest rate of migration in the world" (International Monetary Fund, 2005). Based on the assessments of Memmi (1956), Florida (2002), Runco (2014), and the data from the International Monetary Fund (2005), the Africans in the Caribbean have a destabilized sense of place, which has resulted in socioeconomic crisis. Thus, it seems logical to argue that stabilizing the sense of place for the cultures in the Caribbean is through the intentional assimilation of environments of creative practice.

Intentional environments of creative practice produce solutions of cultural value

Ken Robinson defines creativity as, "the process of having original ideas that have value, more often than not, comes about through the interaction with different disciplinary ways of seeing things" (2006). Recognizing that living systems are comprised of components that represent varied disciplines, an appropriate response to crisis may require originality from alternative perspectives. In order for originality to have the fullest cultural effect, the outcome of the creative practice should not be reduced to solve a specific problem (Csikszentmihalyi, 1988; Runco, 2014). As Lester Brown (2009) stated in his book *Plan b*, "there are solutions to the major problems of our time; some of them even simple, but they require a radical shift in our perceptions, our thinking, our values" (2009). Applying Brown's (2009) logic and Robinson's (2006) definition of creativity to the socioeconomic situation in the Caribbean, valuable solutions to the socioeconomic crisis in the Caribbean can be realized. However, in order for originality to produce solutions of significant cultural value, environments of creative practice must be nurtured and allowed to flourish at all levels of the culture (Runco, 2014).

Summation of intentional environments of creative practice

The expanded theoretical positions in this project indicate that there is a relevant relationship that exists between creative practice and socioeconomic crisis (Figure 4.4). Omitting creative practice as a viable path to socioeconomic growth has had a debilitating affect on the Afro-Carib culture, whereas, intentionally implementing environments of creative practice develops a sustainable path of socioeconomic growth. Noting that the longstanding crisis has affected the reality of life for forty million people in the Caribbean; the political leadership, structures of education, and grassroots organizations have been presented with a decision—keep the cultures in the Caribbean static in socioeconomic crisis or independent in sustainable growth. The first outcome omits the value of creative practice, the second encourages, facilitates, and develops environments of creative practice.

Steeped in ambiguity, creative practice has been "deployed in many different contexts and references many different activities" (Negus and Pickering, 2004, p. vi). The table that follows attempts to comprehensively depict what creative practice is and what creative practice is not based on the analyzed positions in this project (Table 4.2).

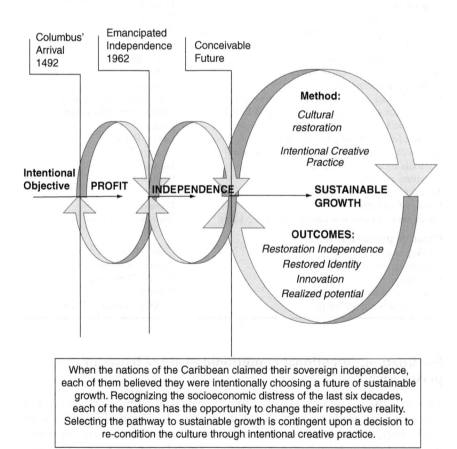

Figure 4.4 The intentional socioeconomic history of the Caribbean and the conceivable future.

Table 4.2 Defining creative practice

Position	Position suggested by
Creative practice is:	
Intentional, a matter of strategic choice	Runco
Source that challenges the rules and conventions	Negus and Pickering
Means to move beyond existing horizons of experience	Negus and Pickering
Means to realized potential	Grugel
Means for understanding a sense of self, forming an identity, meaning	Runco, Grugel, Florida, Capra and Luisi
Means of originality	Capra, Florida, Runco
Driving force of generation and self-generation	Capra and Luisi
Essential to growth	Capra and Luisi
Means for socioeconomic health	Runco, Capra, Rodney
For of vital human capital	Runco
Coping and adaptive mechanism	Runco
Element of survival	Torrance
Essential for producing constructive behavior and unusual achievements	Torrance
Essential for living systems	Capra and Luisi
A constant emergence of novelty	Capra
Means of development	Rodney
Essential phase on the cultural adaptive cycle	Gunderson and Holling
Essential for strength, productivity and health	Gunderson and Holling
Economic stabilizer	James
Catalyst for independence and freedom	James, Runco
Source of resilience, possibilities and renewal	Homer-Dixon
Catalysts to a productive future	Lappe
A natural resource	Guilford
Means to elevate the whole	Guilford
Gauge of stability	Runco
Producer of practical solutions that have value	Brown, Robinson, Runco
Creative practice is not:	
Intelligence	Capra, Runco
Invention, innovation	Runco, Torrance
Discovery	Runco, Torrance
Academic exercise	Runco
Problem-solving technique	Csikszentmihalyi, Runco

Summation: intentional conditioning—three lenses of perspective

The first three chapters of this project—which are my observations and experiences of nearly two decades in the region, the historical progression of the Caribbean, and three theoretical lenses—all seem to emanate consistent themes: oppression, hardship, violence, dependency, underdevelopment, escalating crises, and a strategic cultural conditioning. It should be noted that the themes are not illusionary states solely developed in theoretical discourse;

Table 4.3 Primary topics review

Topic	Key authors	Summary	Connectivity to the Caribbean
Profit Center Theory	Amin, Chilcote, Daly, Girvan, Lewis, Prebisch, Robinson, Shay, Sunkel	Focuses on the influence of a free market/capitalistic model that is strategically designed to develop another region of the world. Through the use of the hegemonic position, the center strategically matures the socioeconomic order through the exploitation of two significant factors, dependency and limitation. Once achieved, the periphery defines the center as their means of survival (dependency), while the center obtains the maximum limits of agriculture and raw materials (limitation). As the periphery is bound to a status quo position of dependency, the center establishes a trajectory of growth through unequal exchange, accumulation, development, and industrialized trade.	The islands of the Caribbean were violently forced into a commercial enterprise through slavery and oppression. Once the imperialistic nations devalued the need for the islands, they implemented an oppressive economic model, which seems to be a source for the current crisis.
Cultural Conditioning Theory	Grugel, Jacques, Kaplan, Klak, Luthar, Memmi, Olwig, Prebisch, Randall, Rodney	Explores the concept of chaos in respect to development, cultural conditioning, and limited land mass. Having strived for independence and development, centuries of culture conditioning toward dependence, and initial conditions embedded in the origin of the culture seem to have contributed to a high level of dependence.	Reasons and outcomes of chaos in relation to dependency in the region. Placed in a position of survival, the islands were forced to submit, which has accentuated crisis.
Intentional Creative Practice Theory	Brown, Capra & Luisi, Florida, Millar, Naipaul, Robinson, Rodney, Runco, Torrance, Walcott	Analyzes the necessity for creative practice within the socioeconomic component of culture. Relinquishing the ownership of life functions create and recreate to another culture has seemingly resulted in crisis. Since a systems view requires a shift in process from the parts to the whole, conscious creative practice is an essential component for living systems that seek survival and achievement.	Essential shift in process is required to ease the hardship. Solutions to the socioeconomic crisis exist, but they might not be realized if the lens of creative practice is not implemented.

they represent the reality of life for forty million people in the Caribbean. Tragically, a path that discounts the reality of the prevailing themes subtly deprives the culture of stability and a sustainable future.

Cumulatively and independently, the three theoretical lenses provide a focused understanding of the socioeconomic crisis in the Caribbean. Utilizing the lenses to define the complex relationship that exists between creative practice and socioeconomic crisis, it seems evident that the strategic suppression of creative practice in the Afro-Carib culture resulted in long-term hardship and crisis. However, the clarity that the lenses provide is not limited to a debilitating problem; they also designate a viable and sustainable path out of socioeconomic crisis. The creative practice lens clarifies the necessity for creativity within all living systems, identifies crises that result from the suppression of creative practice, and expands on the potential outcomes when creative practice is intentionally implemented into political structure and public policy. Thus, a sustainable future for the Afro-Carib culture seems contingent on the restoration of the culture through the intentional implementation of creative practice.

Although the content of the lenses and their respective subdivisions provide focused insight to the relationship between creative practice and socioeconomic crisis the Caribbean, the voice of the people will further validate or reject the respective themes. Through the voice of the people this project seeks to identify "how" and "where" to strategically implement structures of creative practice. The chapter that follows comprehensively analyzes and adheres to the voice of the Afro-Carib culture on St. John, USVI. A further summary of the three lenses is found in Table 4.3.

Notes

1 Magnified Moment #4, in Chapter 2.
2 The Caribbean imported $4.5 billion U.S. dollars of food in 2013. Jamaica accounted for one billion dollars, Trinidad and Tobago imported $950 million, and Haiti imported $903 million. Based on the cumulative population of forty million in the Caribbean, that equates to $112,500 per person of imported food. Even more troubling, $2.5 billion of the imported food was classified "as processed food; yeast and baking powders, stuffed pasta and fast foods" (Sanders, 2014, p. 1).
3 As evident in the relationship between the United Kingdom and the newly independent nations of the Caribbean discussed above, the young nations of the Caribbean assumed that the Lome Agreement would be the source of their social, economic, and political development; instead, their hope of independence and development resulted in a false reality. The Lome Convention is a trade and aid agreement between the European Economic Community (EEC) and 71 African, Caribbean, and Pacific countries signed in 1975 in Lome, Togo. Each of the African, Caribbean, and Pacific countries were former colonies of the British, Dutch, Belgian, and French colonies. The agreement was constructed to secure minerals and agriculture while establishing a quota system for sugar and beef.
4 Magnified Moment #2, in Chapter 2.
5 The majority of the Caribbean nations have adopted a British educational model. The model requires students to take a CXC exam to qualify for high school.

6 The UNODC 2014 report on crime in the Caribbean stated that thirty million tourists visited the region in 2014.

7 Zips (2009) suggested, "Not just the body's and work capability of Africans were 'shipped' to the colonies across the Atlantic, but also their philosophies, ideologies, and knowledge of civilization" (p. 43). Since the Europeans sought to implant the European philosophy, ideology, and civilization into the Africans, a cultural RE-conditioning seems imperative.

8 Magnified Moment #1, in Chapter 2.

9 "Chaos is an orderly disorder"(Gleick, 1987, p. 15).

10 See Lens III: strength through restoration—intentional creative practice.

11 The Royal Bank of the Caribbean Economic Report, March 2016, states that region wide growth continues to sharply fall, the region is highly vulnerable, banking relationships continue to be severed, there is a high threat to the financial sectors and overall economies, grow rates are well below other small island developing nations, productivity is weak, unemployment is among the highest in the world, foreign reserves continue to fall, and debt/GDP ratios are increasing. Retrieved March 2016. (www.rbc.com).

12 The first lens in this project is *Going for the goods—the dark side of capitalism*. The second lens is *Dependence embedded with chaos—cultural conditioning theory*.

13 Runco suggests that creativity is bidirectional, "The concept of directionality applies to the influences on human behavior, including those that contribute to creative potential and creative behavior" (2014, p. 318). The behavioral patterns of leadership are reflected in the behavior of those being governed; whereas, the behavioral patterns of those being governed are also reflected in the leadership. Therefore, the intentional presence of creative practice flows bi-directionally.

14 One of the criticisms of this project is the failure to address political corruptness throughout the Caribbean. Acknowledging that there has been significant political corruptness in the region, there also have been many outstanding political leaders. However, in order for the socioeconomic crisis to ease and implement a strategy of growth, all components of the respective cultures must be participants—including the political leaders.

15 A 1797 law in Barbados made it illegal to teach reading and writing to slaves, a clear indication that the Africans were not wanted for their cognitive process or creative innovations—they were violently accrued for one purpose, their muscles.

16 The criteria for surrendering the "enslaved" asset in the Caribbean, which was a bastion of economic gain for the European continent, required a socioeconomic paradigm shift in both European and Afro-Carib cultures. The political leadership of the imperialistic European nations had to relinquish control over the island cultures. The political leaders of the newly formed Caribbean nations had to construct and implement policies and structures of development. European cultures had to modify their socioeconomic strategies to include new sources of agriculture, raw materials, and labor.

17 IDEO: a global design firm that takes a human-centered, design based approach to helping organizations in the public and private sectors innovate and grow.

18 Self, potential, and place for the Africans in the Caribbean are all central themes that this project is seeking to identify through the voice of the people.

19 While a place's character is a function of physical qualities, it is also a product of risks and opportunities, the nature of the social organization attached to the locale, its political, social, and economic relationships with other places, the psychosocial characteristics of the individuals occupying the space, and the local cultural milieu. We learn to act in specific ways in certain places; we

don't genuflect in bars or drink beer and eat popcorn in churches. Hence, our actions in various places are conditioned by a number of factors, all of which may operate on the individual to affect not only their [*sic*] behavior, but also their [*sic*] health.

(Fitzpatrick, 2000, p. 17)

20 Derek Walcott—Noble Laureate born in St. Lucia. *Dream on Monkey Mountain* was awarded an Obie award in 1971 for the "Best Foreign Play."
21 Being violently displaced from their homeland and relocated to a isolated island void of their cultural practices has had an exponential effect of debilitation—a mandated forfeiture of both a sense of place and a sense of self.
22 Capra (2014) further argues that a key characteristic of life at any level is the reality of change—as organisms change they must maintain their capacity to create or recreate as their source of growth and stability.
23 A comprehensive understanding of the attributes for a *living system* further contextualizes the current and longstanding socioeconomic crises in the Caribbean (Appendix B).

24   Migration has become deeply embedded in the psyche of the Caribbean peoples over the last century and a half. It has evolved as the main avenue for upward mobility through accumulation of capital—financial and social. Thus, the propensity for migration is high and there is a general responsiveness to the opportunities for moving whenever they occur.

(Thomas-Hope, 2000, p. 10)

References

Allen, R. (2006). *Plato: The Republic*. New Haven: Yale University Press.

Amin, S. (1974). *Accumulation on a world scale: A critique of the theory of underdevelopment*. New York, NY: Monthly Review Press.

Bardach, A. (2002). *Cuba confidential: Love and vengeance in Miami and Havana*. New York, NY: Vintage Books.

Bilchitz, D. (2013). Socio-economic rights, economic crisis, and legal doctrine. *International Journal of Constitutional Law*, 12(3): 710–739. DOI: 10.1093/icon/mou044

Blouet, M. (2013). Slavery and freedom n the British West Indies, 1823–33: the role of education. JSTOR, *History of Education Quarterly*, 30(4) (Winter, 1990): 625–643.

Boot, M. (2002). *The savage wars of peace*. New York, NY: Perseus Books.

Brewster, H. (1971). *Economic Dependence*. University of London Institute of Commonwealth Studies, May 1971.

Brown, L. R. (2009). *Plan b 4.0: Mobilizing to save civilization*. New York, NY: Norton.

Brown, L. R. (2011, July 19). Failed States. *Earth Policy Institute*. Retrieved from www.earth-policy.org/images/uploads/press_room/FailedStatesPB.pdf

Capra, F. (2002). *The hidden connections: Integrating the biological, cognitive, and social dimensions of life into a science of sustainability*. New York, NY: Doubleday.

Capra, F., & Luisi, P. (2014). *The systems view of life: A unifying vision*. Cambridge: Cambridge Press.

Caspe, M. (2010, May). Creating environments to promote innovation. *Harvard Family Research Project*, 2(2). Retrieved from www.hfrp.org/publications-resources/browse-our-publications/creating-environments-to-promote-innovation

Caribbean Trade Reference Centre. (n.d.). Lóme and Cotonu agreements. Retrieved from http://ctrc.sice.oas.org/Trade/cotonou/Cotonou.asp

Césaire, A. (1950). *Discourse on colonialism*. New York, NY: Monthly Review Press.

Chilcote, R. (1984). *Theories of development and underdevelopment*. Boulder, CO: Westview Press.

Code Noir [The Black Code]. Liberty, equality, fraternity: Exploring the French revolution. Retrieved from https://chnm.gmu.edu/revolution/d/335/

Collymore, J. (2011). Disaster impact on the Caribbean. Retrieved from http://cdemavl.org/bitstream/123456789/34/1/DISASTER%20IMPACT%20ON%20THE%20CARIBBEAN%20_Collymore%20revised%20in%202001_.pdf

Columbus, C. & Toscanelli, P. (2010) [1893]. Markham, C. (Ed.). *The journal of Christopher Columbus (During hs first voyage)*. London: Cambridge University Press.

Csikszentmihalyl, M. (1996) *Creativity: Flow and the psychology of discovery and invention*, 1st edn. New York, NY: HarperCollins.

Daly, H. E. (2007). *Ecological economics and sustainable development*. Northampton, MA: Edward Elgar.

Davis, C. (1989). *Jamaica in the aluminum industry, 1938–1973* (Vol. 1). Kingston, Jamaica: Kingston Press.

de le Torre, A. (2013). Latin American and the Caribbean as tailwinds recede: In search of higher growth. *The Work Bank*. Retrieved from http://siteresources.worldbank.org/LACINSPANISHEXT/Resources/SM_Report_LatinAmerica_as_Tailwinds_Recede_complete_text_April17_2013concover.pdf

Einhorn, A. (2006). *Indigenous resurgence in the contemporary Caribbean: Amerindian survival and revival*, Forte, A. (Ed.). New York, NY: Peter Lang Publishing.

Florida, R. (2002). *The rise of the creative class: And how it is transforming work, leisure, community and everyday life*. New York, NY: Basic Books.

Focus-Migration (2016, January). Retrieved from www.focus-migration.hwwi.de

Glickman, N., & Harvey, M. (2013). *Culturally affirmative psychotherapy with deaf persons*. New York, NY: Routledge.

Girard, P. (2010). *Haiti: The tumultuous history – From pearl of the Caribbean to broken nation*. New York, NY: St. Martin's Press.

Girvan, N. (2007, July). Towards a single development vision and the role of the single economy. Paper presented at the Twenty-Eighth Meeting of the Conference of Heads of Government on the Caribbean Community, Needham's Point, Barbados.

Girvan, N. (2012, November). Colonialism and neo-colonialism in the Caribbean: An overview. Paper presented at the IV International Seminar Africa, the Caribbean, and Latin America, Kingston, Jamaica. Retrieved from www.normangirvan.info/wp-content/uploads/2013/01/Girvan-St-Vincent-paper.pdf

Girvan, N., & Girvan C. (1973). The development of dependency economics in the Caribbean and Latin America: Review and comparison. *Social and Economic Studies*, 22(1): 1–33. Retrieved from http://sesjournaluwi.blogspot.com

Gleick, J. (1987). *Chaos: Making a new science*. New York, NY: Penguin.

Gmelch, G. (2012). *Beyond the Smile: The working lives of Caribbean tourism*. Bloomington, IN: Indiana University Press.

Grugel, J. (1995). *Politics and development in the Caribbean basin: Central America and the Caribbean in the new world order*. Bloomington, IN: Indiana University Press.

Guilford, P. (1950). Creativity. *American Psychologist*, 5: 444–454.

Gunderson, L., & Holling, C. (2002). *Panarchy: Understanding transformations in human and natural systems*. London: Island Press.

Harvey, D. (2005). *A brief history of neoliberalism*. New York, NY: Oxford University Press.

Hebert, T. P., Cramond, B. L., Speirs Neumeister, K. L., Millar, G., & Silvian, A. F. (2002). *E. Paul Torrance: His life, accomplishments, and legacy.* National Research Center of the Gifted and Talented. (Report No. 02152). Storrs, CT: University of Connecticut.

Henke, H., (2006). *The West Indian Americans.* Westport CT: Greenwood Press.

Higman, B. (2011). *A concise history of the Caribbean.* New York, NY: Cambridge Press.

Hirsch, E., & Walcott, D. (1986). Interviews: Derek Walcott, the art of poetry no. 37. *The Paris Review*, 101. Retrieved from www.theparisreview.org

Homer-Dixon, T. (2006). *The upside of down: Catastrophe, creativity, and the renewal of civilization.* London: Island Press.

International Monetary Fund (2005). Emigration and brain drain: Evidence from the Caribbean. Retrieved from www.imf.org/external/pubs/ft/wp/.../wp0625.pdf

International Monetary Fund (2012, April 12). World economic outlook: Western hemisphere, rebuilding strength and flexibility. Retrieved from www.imf.org/external/pubs/ft/reo/2012/whd/eng/pdf/wreo0412.pdf

Jacques, P. (2015). *Sustainability: The basics.* New York, NY: Routledge.

James, C. L. R. (1983). *At the rendezvous of victory.* London: Allison & Busby.

Jessop, D. (2014). The Caribbean Council. The Caribbean's location is its future. Retrieved from www.caribbean-council.org/the-caribbeans-location-is-its-future/

Kaplan, H. B. (1998). Toward an understanding of resilience: A critical review of definitions and models. In M. D. Glantz & J. L. Johnston (Eds), Resilience and development: Positive life adaptations. New York, NY: Springer Science + Business Media.

Kelshall, G. (1988). *The u-boat war in the Caribbean.* Naval Institute Press.

Klak, T. (1998). *Globalization and neoliberalism: The Caribbean context.* Lanham, MD: Rowan & Littlefield.

Laaksonen, K., Maki-Franti, P., & Virolainen, M. (2010, June 20). Lome convention, agriculture and trade relations between the EU and the ACP countries in 1975–2000. *TRADEAG.* Retrieved from http://ageconsearch.umn.edu/bit-stream/18853/1/wp060020.pdf

Lappe, F. (2011). *Ecomind: Changing the way we think, to create the world we want.* New York, NY: Nation Books.

Lewis, A. (1950). The industrialization of the British West Indies. *Caribbean Economic Review*, 5(50).

Lewis, A. (1954). Economic theories of development: An analysis of competing para-digms. New York, NY: Harvester Wheatsheaf.

Lorenz, E. (1972). Designing chaotic models. *Journal of the Atmospheric Sciences*: Vol. 62, No. 5: 1574–1587.

Luthar, S. S. (2006). Resilience in development: A synthesis of research across five decades. In D. Cicchetti & D. J. Cohen (Eds), *Development psychology* Vol. 3: Risk, disorder, and adaptation (2nd ed.), Hoboken, NJ: John Wiley & Sons, pp. 739–795.

Mackenzie, J. (1990). *Imperialism and the natural world.* Manchester, England: Man-chester University Press.

McIntyre, A. (1964). Some Issues in Trade Policy in the West Indies. In N. Girvan & O. Jefferson (Eds), *Readings in the Political Economy of the Caribbean.* Conference Paper.

McIntyre, A. (1972). Some issues in trade policy in the West Indies. In N. Girvan & O. Jefferson (Eds), *Readings in the political economy of the Caribbean.* Kingston, Jamaica: New World Group.

Meeks, B. (2000). *Narratives of resistance: Jamaica, Trinidad, the Caribbean.* Kingston, Jamaica: University of the West Indies Press.

Memmi, A. (1956). *The colonizer and the colonized.* Boston, MA: Beacon Press.

Memmi, A. (2000). *Racism.* Minneapolis, MN: University of Minnesota Press.

Millar, G. (1995). *E. Paul Torrance: the creativity man.* Norwood, NJ: Ablex.

Naiman, L. (2014). Creativity at work. Retrieved from www.creativityatwork. com/2014/02/17/what-is-creativity/

Naipaul, V. (1969). *The Middle Passage.* New York, NY: Random House.

Negus, K., & Pickering, M. (2004). *Creativity, communication and cultural value.* London: Sage Publications.

Norton, B. (2005). *Sustainability: A philosophy of adaptive ecosystem management.* Chicago, IL: University of Chicago Press.

Olwig, K. F. (1985). *Cultural adaptation and resistance on St. John*: Three centuries of Afro-Caribbean life. Gainesville, FL: University Press of Florida.

Palmie, S. & Francisco, S. (Eds) (2011). *The Caribbean: A history of the region and its peoples.* Chicago, IL: University of Chicago Press.

Pascal, B. (1966). *Pensees* (A. J. Krailsheimer, trans.). Harmondsworth: Penguin.

Payne, A. (1994). *Politics in Jamaica.* New York, NY: St. Martin's Press.

Poincare, H. (1892–1899). *Les methodes nouvelles de la mecanique celeste.* In L. Stewart (2002) *The Lorenz attractor exists.* Nature 406, 948–949.

Prebisch, R. (1951). Growth, disequilibrium and disparities: Interpretation of the process of economic development. *Economic survey of Latin America 1949.* Santiago, Chile: ECLAC.

Prebisch, R. (1980). In R. Chilcote (1984) *Theories of development and underdevelopment.* Boulder, CO: Westview Press.

Proenza-Coles, C. (2006). 1733 St. John Revolt, great events from history: The eighteenth century. Ipswich, MA: Salem Press.

Randall, S., & Mount, G. (1998). *The Caribbean basin: An international history.* London: Routledge.

Robinson, K. (2006, February). How schools kill creativity. *TED.* Retrieved from www.ted.com/talks/ken_robinson_says_schools_kill_creativity?language=en

Rodney, W. (1972). *How Europe underdeveloped Africa.* Baltimore, MD: Black Classic Press. (Original work published 1972).

Royal Caribbean Bank (2016, September). Caribbean economic report. Retrieved from www.rbc.com/economics/economic-data/pdf/Caribbean.pdf

Runco, M. (2014). *Creativity: Theories and themes: Research, development, and practice.* London: Academic Press.

Runco, M., & Jaeger, G. (2012). The Standard Definition of Creativity. *Creative Research Journal*, 24(1): 92–96.

Sachs, I. (1999). Social sustainability and whole development: Exploring the dimensions of sustainable development. In E. Becker and T. Jahn (Eds), *Sustainability and Social Sciences* (London: Zed Books), pp. 25–36.

Sale, K. (1991). *The conquest of paradise: Christopher Columbus and the Columbian legacy.* New York, NY: Plume.

Sanders, R. (2014, June 8). Importing food is damaging the Caribbean: Why no action? Retrieved from www.jamaicaobserver.com

Scott, J. (1990). Domination and the arts of resistance: The hidden transcripts. New Haven, CT: Yale University Press.

Shay, R., Robinson, D., & Cashin, P. (2006). *The Caribbean: From vulnerability to sustained growth*. Washington, DC: International Monetary Fund.

Shepherd, V. (2011, March 28). Obstacles to the Creation of Afrocentric Societies in the Commonwealth Caribbean, Presentation Made to the WGPAD's 10th Session, March 28–April 1, 2011

Strauss, L. (1978). *The city and man*. Chicago, IL: University of Chicago Press.

Sunkel, O., & Girvan, C. (1973). Transnational capitalism and national disintegration in Latin America. *Social and Economic Studies*, 22(1): 132–176.

Tylor, E. B. (1871). *Primitive culture*. New York, NY: Cambridge University Press.

The Library of Congress (1987). Caribbean Islands Social and Economic Developments, 1800-1960. *The Library of Congress*. Retrieved from http://workmall.com/wfb2001/caribbean_islands_history_social_and_economic_developments_1800_1960.html

Thomas–Hope, E. (2000). Trends and Patterns of Migration to and from Caribbean Countries, Sec. 1.2. Retrieved from www.cepal.org

Tierney, H. (1999). *Women's Studies Encyclopedia*, Vol 1. Westport, CT: Greenwood Publishing Group.

Transparency International (2014). Retrieved from www.transparency.org/cpi2014/results

Turner, R. (2014). Travel and Tourism, Economic Impact 2014, *World Travel and Tourism Council*. Retrieved from www.wttc.org/-/media/files/reports/economic%20impact%20research/regional%202015/caribbean2014.pdf

Tylor, E.B. (1871). *Primitive culture*. New York, NY: Cambridge University Press.

UNICEF (2013). UNICEF Annual report 2013-Eastern Caribbean multi-country programme. Retrieved from www.unicef.org

UNODC (2014). Global Status Report on Violence Prevention. Retrieved from www.undp.org/content/dam/undp/library/corporate/Reports/UNDP-GVA-violence-2014.pdf

Walcott, D. (1969). *The Gulf*. New York, NY: Macmillan Press.

Walcott, D. (1970). *Dream on Monkey Island*, New York, NY: Macmillan Press.

Walcott, D. (1984). *Midsummer: XXVII*. New York, NY: Macmillan Press.

Williams, E. (1993). *Eric E. Williams speaks: Essays on Colonialism and Independence*. Wellesley, MA: Calaloux Publishing.

Wolf, E. (2010). *Europe and the people without history*. Berkeley, CA: University California Press.

World Bank Group (2015). The world bank. Retrieved from www.worldbank.org

World Health Organization (2014, December). Global status report on violence prevention 2014. Retrieved from www.who.int/violence_injury_prevention/violence/status_report/2014/en/

Zavala, M. (2013). What do you mean by decolonizing research strategies? Lessons from decolonizing, indigenous research projects in New Zealand and Latin America. *Decolonization: Indigeneity, Education & Society*, 2(1): 55–71.

Zips, W. (2009). *Black rebels: African Caribbean freedom fighters in Jamaica*. Princeton, NJ: Markus Weiner.

5 Amplifying the Afro-Carib voice—research design and methodology

Through imperialistic decree, the Afro-Carib voice was strategically suppressed and intentionally ignored for more than five centuries (Zips, 2009).[1] Thus, the remaining content of this project methodically respects the humanity of the culture by prioritizing the voice of the people. Although well-intentioned scholars have theoretically analyzed the hardship in the Caribbean, the voice of the Afro-Carib culture is essential to understanding the meaning and texture of the socioeconomic phenomenon in the region (Creswell, 2007). Utilizing a phenomenological research model to accurately amplify the Afro-Carib voice, the model "is used to obtain knowledge about how we think and feel in the most direct ways" (Bentz & Shapiro, 1998, p. 96). To further develop the relationship between creative practice and socioeconomic crisis in the Caribbean, this chapter will illuminate the *thoughts and feelings* of the Afro-Carib culture *in the most direct ways*. Further, this chapter expands on the rationale, design, and research methodology to accurately amplify the voice of the Afro-Carib people (Creswell, 2013).

Historical rationale for respecting the Afro-Carib voice

The Afro-Caribs have been engaged in a longstanding struggle to identify and articulate their cultural identity (Zips, 2009). Rodney (1972) suggests that intentionally suppressed voices motivate acts of resistance, which can result in tragic outcomes.[2] The historical progression of the region corroborates Rodney's (1972) position and illuminates the sacrifice required to "be heard" in a violently suppressed environment—as the following corroborates, when the Afro-Carib voices were muted, resistance and revolt was formed.

When a slave named Toussaint L' Ouverture demanded that the French acknowledge the Afro-Carib voice in St. Domingue, the French refused and a revolution ensued (James, 1938).[3] The revolution ended in 1801 with more than 150,000 Afro-Caribs killed (James, 1938). In Jamaica, a group of Afro-Caribs concluded they could no longer keep their voice repressed, the revolt in 1760 resulted in more than 500 Afro-Caribs killed, executed, or committing suicide (Brown, 2012). Sixty years later, another revolt in

Jamaica ended with 300 slaves killed and another 300 hanged for their role in the revolt (Andrews, 2013). In Trinidad, when the *Code Noir*[4] outlawed the African expressions of dance and drumming in 1685, the suppression of voice became the catalyst for reoccurring slave revolts for the next 100 years (Williams, 1944).

In the context of St. John, Virgin Islands, Andrews (2013) suggests that the 1733 slave revolt was one of the seven worst slave rebellions ever documented. The revolt was the product of inhumane brutality and an intentionally suppressed voice (Olwig, 1985). When imperialistic powers united to overpower the St. John slave revolt, many of the Afro-Caribs chose suicide over further hardship, murder, and mandated silence (Dookhan, 1996). Tragically, it seems that suicide was seen as a better alternative than a muted voice. Allain (2014) stated that Afro-Carib mothers often committed infanticide with the "intentions of the saving their children from slavery and resisting slaveholding hegemony" (p. 1).

The historical account of the region reveals that the Afro-culture suffered greatly fighting to be heard. The intentional suppression of voice of the people resulted in crisis and isolation of the most deplorable kind. Thus, it seems plausible to suggest that the struggle for the voice of the Caribbean cultures to "be heard" remains as a relevant source of socioeconomic crisis in the region.

Observed rationale for the Afro-Carib voice

My experiences as a fulltime resident in the Caribbean corroborate the extensive struggle and methods to "be heard" by the Afro-Carib culture. When the Rastafarian in Jamaica stood on the road in front of the school yelling disparaging insults at me for over a year—could it be that he chose an extreme method to be heard?[5] When the thieves held me at gunpoint beside the Rio Cobre River—were they using crime as a method to be heard?[6] When the farmers in York Castle, Jamaica asked me to meet with them, they were desperate to have their voice heard.[7] In the context of St. John, I witnessed angry protestors burn down the Meade building in downtown Cruz Bay in September 2005—were the protestors using violence as a method to be heard?

For five centuries the Afro-Carib culture has been forced to embrace extreme methods to have their voice heard—why is it so difficult to respectfully listen to the voice of the people and work together ease socioeconomic hardship for the Afro-Carib culture? The remaining content of this project attempts to un-suppress the voice of the Afro-Caribs to further identify the texture and meaning of everyday life, analyze the reality of socioeconomic crisis, and develop a path of sustainable growth.[8] In an effort to fully respect the voice of the culture, this project utilized the following research methodology and approaches to amplify the Afro-Carib voice.

Methodology: qualitative method

Utilizing a qualitative method to establish distinct research guidelines, this project began with a designated phenomenon reflected in a primary research question (Creswell, 2013). The phenomenon of long-term socioeconomic hardship for the Afro-Carib culture serves as the motivation for the primary research question in this project, "What is the relationship between creative practice and socioeconomic crisis in the Caribbean?" Thus, to accurately define the phenomenon through a deep description of lived experience and meaning, the qualitative method was essential (Patton, 2002). A contrasting method would be the quantitative approach, one that seeks a high volume of participants in order to achieve a broader understanding of the phenomenon. Although the method is appropriate in many subjects of research, the high volume of participants constrains the outcomes to a surface understanding, one that is devoid of the deep texture of everyday reality that this project is seeking.

The structural components of the qualitative method are designed to secure the characteristics of a phenomenon beyond biased appearances (Leedy & Ormrod, 2010). The qualitative components of setting and participation are critical factors that are directly correlated to accuracy, population variability, and thorough data analysis (Neuman, 2006). Therefore, as Creswell (2013) and Neuman (2006) suggest, the participant size must be limited to a small number in order to define the texture of reality. The participation size for this project is sixteen participants from the Afro-Carib culture.

Selecting the setting for data collection is equally as important as the quantity of participants (Neuman, 2006). The qualitative process requires the collection of information "in a natural setting sensitive to the people and places" (Creswell, 1999, p. 44). To satisfy this criterion I captured the Afro-Carib voice by respecting setting and place through one-on-one conversational interviews—each participant selected their *natural setting* for their respective interview on St. John, U.S.V.I. According to Creswell (2013), successful outcomes and relevant data from qualitative interviews satisfy the objective of the qualitative method, which is to obtain the current reality of life from the members in the community through ontological, epistemological, and axiological positions—the ontology, epistemology, and axiology positions were respected and fulfilled in this project.

Ontology

Noting that the ontological position "relates to the reality and its characteristics" (Creswell, 2013, p. 20), one-on-one conversational interviews provide the freedom to express perceptions and feelings that reflect the individual and their shared reality (Sherrod, 2006). As Creswell (2013) notes, the only method to provide an accurate description of life is through the one who has lived it; however, an ontological approach reaches beyond a description to identify the meaning of the phenomenon. Analyzing the data from the interviews through open and axial coding allowed me to identify, organize, and illuminate the connections that define the shared meaning of life for the participants (Shank, 2006; Moustakas, 1994). The variance outcomes further produced a broad and clear reality through the developed themes (Creswell, 2013). The themes, in the context of the socioeconomic crisis and the role of creative practice in the Caribbean, provide an ontological element of clarity for the findings in this project.

Epistemology

Creswell (2013) suggested that validating an epistemological assumption is established through the degree of closeness between the investigator and the participant(s). In order to establish the depth of closeness required, I dedicated six weeks in September of 2015 to conduct sixteen one-on-one conversational interviews (Wolcott, 2008). Five sequential steps were implemented to serve as a filter to ensure closeness and secure firsthand information from the participants: (1) a personal relationship with each of the participants; (2) face-to-face conversations with each participant to explain the study; (3) a two week reflection period—to confidently determine participation; (4) complete and receive permission forms from each participant to conduct a one-on-one conversational interview; and (5) conduct the interviews in a place of convenience and comfort for each respective participant.

Axiology

Acknowledging that I have resided in the community of St. John, Virgin Islands for ten years and resided in the region for nearly two decades, I have established biases and values that reflect the Afro-Carib culture. Although my positionality and the subsequent bias positions were instrumental in recognizing the phenomenon, Leedy and Ormrod (2010) suggest that bias is the greatest threat to qualitative inquiry. Therefore, in an effort to substantiate the findings of this project and facilitate credibility, I have accentuated my transparent positionality and biasness in this project. The Magnified Moments in this project are an expansion of my positionality—my stated biases are found in the introduction to the literature review in this project.[9] Further, Morgan and Dury (2003) argue that minimized bias and reliable outcomes are contingent on detailed documentation of data collection, applied methodology, and interpretation of meaning, all of which have been implemented and expanded on in this project.

Ethical considerations

As previously stated in Chapter 2, I acknowledge and recognize that I am a Caucasian man with ontological roots in Atlanta, Georgia. Acknowledging that the one-on-one interviews were conducted solely with Afro-Carib people, this project was submitted and approved by the Prescott College Institutional Review Board prior to the interviews—ethical approval was granted prior to any data collection. Recognizing a cultural and racial difference between myself and participants, sensitivity to the difference served as the highest priority in this project. Following scheduled face-to-face meetings with each participant to discuss the project and gather demographic data (Table 5.1), all participants were provided with Informed Consent forms in which they voluntarily accepted or declined participation in the study—all sixteen participants accepted the invitation to participate in this project. Since the participants of this research will remain anonymous, the last names of the participants were not recorded on any research documentation (consent forms are the only exception). The participants are only identified by a numerical value—the names of the participants were not used in the publication of this project.

Identifying experiences and meanings: the Afro-Carib lifeworld

This project was generated through an observed phenomenon, not a theory (Simon & Goes, 2011). I selected phenomenology to "explicate the meaning, structure, and essence of the lived experience" for the Afro-Carib culture suffering through long-term socioeconomic crisis in the Caribbean (Christensen, Johnson, & Turner, 2010, p. 4). Accurately identifying the meanings and experiences of the phenomenon required more than observations, historical progressions, and theoretical analyses—a phenomenology study analyzes the structural intentionally of the phenomenon through a first person point of view (Rehorick & Bentz, 2008). I reached for a "rich and vivid account" of why the culture is experiencing hardship (Vaill, 1978, p. 119) by "uncovering the meaning of *lived experience* within an *everyday lifeworld*" (Rehorick & Bentz, 2008, p. 3).

Table 5.1 Demographic survey

Information	Response
First name	
Contact information (preferred way for follow up communication), text, email, telephone, and/or address.	
Age	
Are you an Afro-Carib living on St. John, U.S. Virgin Islands for a minimum of 5 years?	YES/NO
Are you freely willing to participate in a one-on-one conversational interview and follow up focus group in order to discuss the relationship between creativity and socioeconomic crisis in the Caribbean?	YES/NO

To confirm the selection of phenomenology for this project, I examined the methodology, approaches, and findings chapters of three Ph.D. dissertations. Each of the research projects utilized the parameters of phenomenology to collect and interpret data (Table 5.2). The projects allowed me to ascertain a deeper understanding of the phenomenological process and structure. The research projects are as follows.

All three projects accentuate similar structural components; a participant sample that is purposeful and small in size, one-on-one conversational interviews, theme development through coding, and findings formed through firsthand accounts of meanings and experiences. According to Patton (2002), purposeful sampling is necessary for a project that seeks to deepen the understanding of a phenomenon and learn about the real life experiences of the participants. Since the participants are the "experiential experts of the phenomenon" (Rudestam & Newton, 2001, p. 92), it is imperative to select participants who have experienced the reality of the phenomenon (Rudestam & Newton, 2001).[10] Further, a purposeful sampling sufficiently represents the population of study in order to yield the most relevant information about the topic (Leedy & Ormrod, 2010). Newman (2006) noted that the objective of the qualitative project is to comprehensively understand the phenomenon. Based on the three noted projects, a small sampling size facilitated depth to the one-on-one interviews and provided meaning and understanding to the current lifeworld experienced by the Afro-Carib culture.

Community selection—satisfying the criteria of voice

Legitimizing the voices of those who have been historically excluded, which are race/gender, economically marginalized, and disabled is a key component of the qualitative method (Bentz & Rehorick, 2008). This project accentuates the voice that reflects the everyday lives of a marginalized culture in the

Table 5.2 Qualitative research projects

Title of project	Author	Number of participants	Method used to establish meaning
The Revolting Self: An Interpretative Phenomenological Analysis of the Experience of Self-Disgust in Females with Depressive Symptoms	Powell, P., Overton, P., & Simpson, J.	9	One-on-One conversational interviews
Phenomenological study of lived experiences of Congolese refuges resettled in the United States	Twagiramungu, E.	20	One-on-One conversational interviews & focus groups
The Experience of Living Kidney Donors: Disenfranchised grief before, during, and after donation.	Young, V.	12	One-on-One conversational interviews

Caribbean. Yielding to the qualitative phenomenology criteria, I constructed a platform of "voice" that represents the Afro-Carib culture throughout the region—a narrative that reflects the reality of everyday life by "exploring real life within a contemporary context or setting" (Creswell, 2013, p. 97).

The community I selected to represent a contemporary context for the Afro-Carib culture is St. John, United States Virgin Islands. The island meets the qualitative criteria of a "culture-sharing group" for seven reasons (Creswell, 2013, p. 94). First, as a ten-year resident and educator in the Virgin Islands, I experienced and witnessed socioeconomic hardship. Second, due to historically poor economies throughout the Caribbean, Afro-Caribs have migrated to the Virgin Islands to earn U.S. dollars in order to send back to their home islands. As a result of the migration, the Virgin Islands have become a point of convergence for the Afro-Carib culture—unlike the majority of the Caribbean nations, many of the island nations are represented on St. John. Third, the island is economically dependent on the hegemonic power of the United States. Economic dependency on hegemonic powers seems to be an inhibitor of sustainable growth throughout the region. Fourth, St. John has one of the highest ratios of expatriates in the Caribbean, which has created a cultural crisis between the Afro-Caribs and the expatriates. Fifth, St. John is an ideal representation of the historical progression of the Caribbean. The indigenous people group—Taíno Indians—were victims of a strategic act of genocide (Olwig, 1985). The remnants of their culture can be found throughout the Virgin Islands. The Afro-Caribs were violently imported to serve as a labor force to advance imperialistic initiatives on St. John (Andrews, 2013). The remnants of the sugar cane factories and the plantation society litter the island.[11] Furthermore, the Afro-Carib culture on St. John has struggled to discover a unique cultural identity through development and neoliberalism periods due to economic dependency on the United States. Last, grassroots creativity seems to abound on the island. Due to the high cost of living and economic instability, people are forced to make repairs to their homes, transportation, and general wellbeing from items that other cultures discard. Cultural creativity, art, and music are plentiful, yet creativity of all forms seems to be compartmentalized in a sphere of survival.

In sum, as an island in the Caribbean, St. John is an appropriate site for this project due to its historical socio-economic hardship, cultural diversity, historical context, and creative initiative for survival. St. John possesses the necessary components to be a microcosm of the Caribbean, which makes it an ideal location to construct meaning from the reality of everyday life (Patton, 2002).

Selection of participants

Reaching for a voice that accurately reflects the reality of everyday life for the Afro-Carib culture, I requested the participation of sixteen Afro-Carib people from distinct demographical spheres on St. John, U.S. Virgin Islands. The demographical spheres include six eighth grade students from Julius E. Sprauve School, one school guidance counselor, one member of the Department of Education administration, one barge captain, one employee of the National Park, one government employee, one sole proprietor, one human resource director, and three employees from diverse areas in the tourism sector (Table 5.3). The sixteen participants were equally segmented—eight females and eight males.[12] The criteria for strategically selecting the participants for this research project are as follows; (a) an Afro-Carib resident of St. John, U.S. Virgin Islands five years or longer; (b) willing to complete the pre-research documentation as mandated by Prescott College and the International Review Board; and (c) participate in one 60–90 minute conversational interview with the primary investigator. Once the criteria was agreed upon, the participant was asked to complete a demographic survey (Table 5.1) and all of the respective consent forms for their demographic sphere—Informed Consent, Minor's Assent, Parent/Legal Guardian Consent, and/or Site Authorization.

Pilot interviews

To sufficiently prepare for the sixteen conversational interviews and ensure effective outcomes, I conducted four pilot interviews in May 2015 (Table 5.3).

Table 5.3 Participant demographics

P	Age (years)	Sex	St. John resident	Residency (years)	Afro-Carib	Occupation
1	14	F	Y	14	Y	Student
2	14	M	Y	14	Y	Student
3	14	F	Y	14	Y	Student
4	14	M	Y	14	Y	Student
5	14	M	Y	14	Y	Student
6	14	F	Y	14	Y	Student
7	51	F	Y	51	Y	Dept. of Education
8	33	M	Y	33	Y	Government employee
9	27	F	Y	22	Y	Tourism sector
10	50	F	Y	50	Y	Dept. of Education
11	38	F	Y	24	Y	Human resources
12	46	M	Y	32	Y	Barge captain
13	41	M	Y	26	Y	Hotel employee
14	31	F	Y	31	Y	Tourism sector
15	22	M	Y	22	Y	National park employee
16	40	M	Y	36	Y	Sole proprietor

Pilot participants' demographics

P	Age	Sex	St. John resident	Residency	Afro-Carib	Occupation
1	38	F	Y	38	Y	Musician
2	37	M	Y	37	Y	Utility worker
3	39	F	Y	26	Y	Administrative Asst.
4	59	M	Y	45	Y	V.I. Court

Each of the interviews took place on St. John, V.I. at a location determined by the participant. I strategically arranged the pilot interviews to emulate the conditions and interactions of the interviews to be conducted in the fall of 2015 (Douglas, 1985). Four pilot interviews allowed me to refine the interview questions, develop effective follow-up questions, and evaluate the nuances of recording and note taking.

A first person point of view: one-on-one conversational interviews

In an effort to comprehensively analyze the socioeconomic phenomenon and explore the relationship between creative practice and socioeconomic crisis in the Caribbean, I reached for a shared understanding of the reality of life as it pertains to the participants (Creswell, 2013). To sufficiently expand my understanding, I utilized one-on-one conversational interviews "to enter into the other person's perspective (Patton, 2002, p. 341).[13] Reaching for trustworthy and valuable data from the interviews, I adhered to Simon and Goes' (2011, p. 4) process for conversation interviews.

(1) Identify the appropriate approach to ask questions.
(2) Have a well-developed set of questions that answer the research question.
(3) Ask direct questions first, then follow up question(s).
(4) Clarify when there is doubt or unclear statements.
(5) Maintain professionalism and respect by being a patient and active listener.

Prior to the interviews, I spent a month developing the research questions to be asked to each participant, followed by feedback and approval from two respected qualitative researchers, Dr(s) Pramod Parajuli and Kim Langmaid. The twelve questions and seven follow-up questions were designed to amplify the Afro-Carib voice related to four central themes—sense of self, sense of place, socioeconomic crisis, and creative practice (Table 5.4). Each theme is equally represented in the interview questions.

Each of the sixteen participants chose a setting for the interviews and was respectively asked identical questions (Creswell, 2013). The one-on-one interviews represent participants from nine distinct Afro-Carib demographical spheres on St. John, U.S.V.I. The objective of each interview was to illuminate hidden themes and key characteristics from the reality of everyday life on the island. The outcomes of the one-on-one interviews provide descriptive themes and characteristics of the phenomenon and expose a potential pathway to sustainable growth—a path that could diffuse the longstanding socioeconomic crisis in the region and establish a true identity.

Table 5.4 SPEC assessment

Location:

Participant number:

Question	Theme	Anticipated response	Follow up item	Notes:
1. Tell me how you think your everyday experiences on St. John differ from everyday experiences on the mainland.	Sense of place			
2. If you could sum up West Indian life on St. John in one word, what would that word be?	Sense of place	Paradise, beautiful, difficult, hardship, relational	Why does your term best describe St. John?	
3. From your perspective, tell me what it means to be a West Indian living on St. John?	Sense of self	Quiet, blessed, hard, difficult,		
4. How do you feel about the current economic situation in the territory? How does it affect your everyday life?	Socioeconomic Sense of Place Sense of Self	Food, energy, and overall quality of life	Would you consider the current economic situation a crisis? If so, why is it a crisis?	
5. Describe in detail how the West Indian culture on St. John has been most affected by the economic situation?	Socioeconomic Place	Food costs, energy costs, quality of life	Do you believe you have the power to change those things? If so, how?	
6. If you could add a subject of priority into the schools, what would the subject be?	Creative/Innovative Place	Vocational trades	Tell me why you think the subject would make things better for future generations of West Indians?	

#	Question	Code		Follow-up
7.	Let's change subjects … Tell me about classes in school that allowed you to be creative.	Creative	Varied	Where you creative on your own or did the instructor invite you to be creative?
8.	Describe in detail what kind of creativity you have witnessed on St. John.	Creativity		
9.	Tell me about the last time you were creative. What did you create? Why did you create it?	Creativity		Do you feel you have the proper tools or training to be creative in the Virgin Islands? If not, describe to me what you would change.
10.	When you feel creative, describe for me what you like to create?	Creative/Innovative Place	Yes, the cost to live is prohibitive.	Describe to me why you believe it is realistic or unrealistic to create something that would positively change the lives of West Indians throughout the Virgin Islands.
11.	Describe for me in detail how creativity influences the economy of the Virgin Islands.	Creative, Socioeconomic		
12.	Describe for me the role of creativity in moving forward for the West Indian culture.	Creative		

Creative practice: additional objective for one-on-one interviews

Having identified the necessity and benefits for the presence of creative practice within the socioeconomic component of the Afro-Carib culture, six of the interview questions were designed to assess the value and environment of creative processes within the Afro-Carib culture. As Runco (2014) argued, "determining 'How an individual can be creative?' leads to a creative process and is tied to explanations of motivation and creative intentions" (p. 318). Thus, this project identifies factors that suppress and motivate creative intentions in the Afro-Carib culture.[14] To accomplish these objectives, this project examined a "complexity of views" (Creswell, 2013) by capturing the Afro-Carib voice, collecting data, and interpreting the findings.

Analysis and interpretation

The qualitative data derived from the sixteen conversational interviews included audio recordings, transcripts, and my handwritten interview notes. Each of the collected components was organized in Microsoft Word documents and NVivo 10 nodes[15] in effort to comprehensively illuminate shared meaning and themes of experience—the recorded interviews were transcribed verbatim. Additionally, the transcripts were repetitively analyzed in concert with my notes and recordings to assure an accurate reproduction of the Afro-Carib voice.

The NVivo software allowed me to analyze the data through open and axial coding, which is essential for qualitative phenomenological research (Shank, 2006). Coding is a comprehensive process that allows the investigator to organize, create, and visualize emerging themes from in-depth conversational interviews. Holton (2010) states, "open coding forces researchers to verify and saturate categories, minimizes the omission of an important category, and ensures relevance by generating codes with an emergent fit to the substantive area under study" (p. 25). While the open coding process is focused on the text generated from the interviews, axial coding assures that the relationship between the themes and concepts accurately depict the interview (Creswell, 2013). In respect to this project, the NVivo platform facilitated data analysis, relational organization, category designation, and pattern illumination (Bergin, 2011).

Analytic process

Utilizing phenomenological data analysis procedures developed by Smith, Flowers and Larkin (2009), Van Manen (1990), and Creswell (2007), the data collected from the sixteen interviews followed a six phase analytic process (Van Manen, 1990, pp. 92–96).

- Phase one: Active engagement
  Active engagement with the data is essential for qualitative researchers (Creswell, 2013). The data collected from the interviews was read and re-read prior to any cross case analysis. This phase included highlighting any information that seemed relevant to the central research question of this project.
- Phase two: Exploratory notation
  The transcripts were notated with comments that accentuated descriptive moments, events, linguistic clarity, and conceptual features of the conversation.
- Phase three: Holistic review
  The general meanings of highlighted passages were identified and articulated in a sentence format.

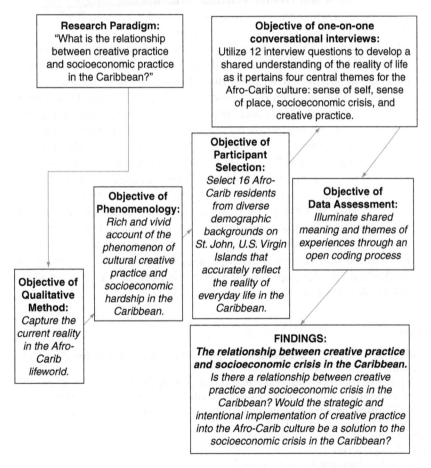

Figure 5.1 Research paradigm: the relationship between creativity and socioeconomic crisis in the Caribbean.

- Phase four: Selective review
  This phase marks the beginning of the phenomenological reduction (Moustakas, 1994). Key phases revealing significant aspects of the phenomenon were highlighted and bracketed into, "Delimited Horizons or Meanings—horizons that stand out as invariant qualities of the experience" (Moustakas, 1994, p. 180). The filter for this phase was the designation of "non-repetitive, non-overlapping themes" (Moustakas, 1994, p. 180).
- Phase five: Detailed review
  Sentence clusters and paragraphs were evaluated for meaning followed by theme assignment. The themes were divided into one of two categories; "textural or structural" (Creswell, 2007, p. 62). The *textural* experiences in this project are designated as a transformative experience—i.e., socio-economic crisis and creative practice.[16] The *structural* category describes the context in which the phenomenon occurred (Creswell, 2007).
- Phase six: Thematic composite descriptions
  The content of the Findings section for a phenomenology study is developed in phase six. A "draft of the textural and structural descriptions generate a composite description that identifies essential, invariant structures of the phenomenon" (Creswell, 2007, p. 62). Moustakas (1994) states that textural descriptions begin with the individual—integrated, descriptive, invariant constituents that are developed through accentuated horizons, non-repetitive, non-overlapping clusters, and themes that represent each participant (p. 180). Individual textural descriptions are followed by composite textural descriptions—"an integration of all of the individual textural descriptions into a group or universal textural description" (Moustakas, 1994, p. 180). Structural themes are developed through the context of time, space, relationship to self, to others, bodily concerns, causal and intentional structures. Following the composite descriptions for textural and structural descriptions, the two types of themes are synthesized to develop meaning and essences of the phenomenon (Moustakas, 1994, p. 181).

Notes

1　Refer to Chapter 3 for a detailed analysis on the suppression of the Afro-Carib culture.
2　A point of reference outside the region that possibly influenced the methods that the imperialistic nations used to silent the Afro-Caribs—to keep the slaves silent, the "Spartans declared war on their slaves each year to frighten them into submission" (Andrews, 2013, p. 1).
3　St. Domingue is modern day Haiti.
4　Refer to Chapter 3.
5　Magnified Moment #6, in Chapter 2.
6　Magnified Moment #1, in Chapter 2.
7　Magnified Moment #4, in Chapter 2.

8 Following a conference in Miami, Florida focused on the Caribbean, Paul Walker, PhD said to me,

> A nugget of truth can be found in all forms of criticism, those who find the nugget and modify their behavior will rise above all levels of expectation, but those who selfishly refuse to listen for the nugget of truth isolate themselves in a destructive way of life.
>
> (Walker, 2000)

9 The Literature Review in this project is to be found in Chapter 4.
10 Refer to the Selection of Participants section in this chapter.
11 Andrews (2013) suggests that the 1733 slave revolt was one of the seven worst slave rebellions ever documented. The revolt was the product of inhumane brutality and an intentionally suppressed voice (Olwig, 1985).
12 Julius S. Sprauve School is a government school primary school located in Cruz Bay, St. John, U.S. Virgin Islands.
13 The five steps for securing the sixteen participants are located in the *Epistemology* section of this chapter.
14 As a participant of life in the Caribbean for nearly two decades, I have observed an inferiority complex that seems to be a residual effect of nearly 500 years of slavery. Therefore, many Afro-Carib residents of the Caribbean seem to believe that creativity is reserved specifically for the gifted. As Negus and Pickering (2004) have suggested,

> As creativity has acquired its modern meanings, it has become associated with beliefs that can be construed as both elitists and essentialist. Elitist conceptions of creativity assume that only some people have the potential to be or become creative and only certain forms of creativity really matter, while essentialist assumptions lead to beliefs that certain types of creativity are a natural gift of biological or social science.
>
> (p. 115)

For this reason and others, it is imperative for this research to include the voice of the Afro-Carib culture.
15 NVivo nodes

> are a collection of references about a specific theme or case. You gather the references by "coding" sources to a node. There are different types of nodes in the NVivo software that represent the themes and cases in the project. Theme nodes are for source material. Case nodes are the units of observation that include people, places, sites or organizations.
>
> (www.nvivo.com)

16 *Transformative experience*—possess two traits of dimension; epistemically and personal. "an experience that provides knowledge that is epistemically inaccessible to the knower until he or she has that experience." The personal dimension is an experience that transforms self, the subject preferences, or the epistemic states of a knower in some deep perhaps even unpredictable way" (Philosophy of Transformative Experience, 2016, p. 1).

References

Allain, J. (2014, January). Infanticide as Slave Resistance: Evidence from Barbados, Jamaica, and Saint-Dominique. *Student Pulse*. Retrieved from www.studentpulse.com

Andrews, E. (2013, January). Seven famous slave revolts. History lists. Retrieved from www.history.com/news/history-lists/7-famous-slave-revolts

Bentz, V., & Shapiro, J. (1998). *Mindful inquiry in social research*. Thousand Oaks, CA: Sage Publications.

Bergin, M. (2011, April). NVivo 8 and consistency in data analysis: Reflecting on the use of a qualitative data analysis program. *ResearchGate*, 18(3): 6–12. DOI:10.7748/nr2011.04.18.3.6.c8457.

Brown, V. (2012). Slave Revolt in Jamaica, 1760–1761: A Cartographic Narrative. Retrieved from www.revolt.axismaps.com

Christensen, L., Johnson, R., & Turner, L. (2010). *Research methods design and analysis* (11th ed.). Boston, MA: Allyn & Bacon.

Creswell, J. (2007). *Qualitative inquiry & research design: Choosing among five approaches*. London: Sage Publications.

Creswell, J. (2013). *Qualitative inquiry & research design: Choosing among five approaches* (2nd ed.). London: Sage Publications.

Dookhan, I. (1996). *A Pre-Emancipation History of the West Indies*. London: Longman Group U.K., Ltd.

Douglas, J. (1985). *Creative Interviewing*. London: Sage Publications.

Holton, J. (March, 2010). The coding process and its challenges. *Grounded Theory Review: An International Journal*, 9. Retrieved from http://groundedtheoryreview.com/2010/04/02/the-coding-process-and-its-challenges/

James, C. L. R. (1938). *The black jacobins*. London: Secker & Warburg.

Leedy, P., & Ormrod, J. (2010). *Practical Research*. Upper Saddle River, NJ: Merrill.

Morgan, A., & Dury, V. (December 2003). Legitimising the subjectivity of human reality through qualitative research method. *ResearchGate*. Retrieved from: www.researchgate.net/publication/49284078_Legitimising_the_Subjectivity_of_Human_Reality_Through_Qualitative_Research_Method

Moustakas, C. (1994). *Phenomenological Research Methods*. London: Sage Publications.

Neuman, W. (2006). *Social research methods: Qualitative and quantitative approaches*. Toronto, CA: Pearson.

Olwig, K. F. (1985). *Cultural adaptation and resistance on St. John: Three centuries of Afro-Caribbean life*. Gainesville, FL: University Press of Florida.

Patton, M. Q. (2002). *Qualitative research & evaluation methods*. London: Sage Publications.

Philosophy of transformative experience (2016). *University of Notre Dame Center of Philosophy of Religion*. Retrieved from http://philreligion.nd.edu/research-initiatives/the-experience-project/philosophy-of-transformative-experience/

Powell, P. A., Overton, P. G., & Simpson, J. (Eds) (2015). *The revolting self: Perspectives on the psychological, social, and clinical implications of self-directed disgust*. London: Karnac Books.

Rehorick, D., & Bentz, V. (2008). *Transformative phenomenology: Changing ourselves, lifeworlds, and professional practice*. Plymouth: Lexington Books.

Rodney, W. (1972). *How Europe underdeveloped Africa*. Baltimore, MD: Black Classic Press. (Original work published 1972).

Rudestam, K., & Newton, R. (2001). *Surviving your dissertation: A comprehensive guide to content and process*. London: Sage Publications.

Runco, M. (2014). *Creativity: Theories and themes: Research, development, and practice*. London: Academic Press.

Shank, G. (2006). *Qualitative research: A personal skills approach*. New York, NY: Pearson.

Sherrod, L. (2006). Promoting citizenship and activism in today's youth. In S. Ginwright, & R. Watts (Eds), *Beyond resistance! Youth activism and community change: New democratic possibilities for practice and policy for America's children*. New York, NY: Routledge.

Simon, M., & Goes, J. (2011). What is phenomenological research? Retrieved from http://dissertationrecipes.com/wp-content/uploads/2011/04/Phenomenological-Research.pdf

Smith, J. A., Flowers, P., & Larkin, M. (2009). *Interpretative phenomenological analysis: Theory, method and research*. London: Sage.

Twagiramungu, E. (2013). A phenomenological study of lived experiences of Congolese refugees resettled in the United States. PhD Thesis. Phoenix, AZ, University of Phoenix. Retrieved from http://search.proquest.com/docview/1552487189

Vaill, P. (1978). Toward a Behavioral Description of High Performing Systems. In Morgan McCall, & Michael Lombardo (Eds), *Leadership: Where else can we go?* Durham, NC: Duke University Press, pp. 103–125.

Van Manen, M. (1990). *Researching lived experience*. Canada: The Althouse Press.

Williams, E. (1944). *Capitalism and slavery*. Chapel Hill, NC: University of North Carolina Press.

Wolcott, H. (2008). *Ethnography: A way of seeing*. New York, NY: Alta Mira Press.

Young, V. (2007). The experience of living kidney donors. Disenfranchised grief, before, during and after donation. PhD Thesis. Santa Barbara, Fielding Graduate University.

Zips, W. (2009). *Black rebels: African Caribbean freedom fighters in Jamaica*. Princeton, NJ: Markus Weiner.

6 Emergent themes—participant generated findings

The purpose of this project is to analyze the relationship between creative practice and socioeconomic crisis in the Caribbean. In order to ascertain the meanings and lived experiences of the Afro-Carib culture, the *findings* component of this project was captured through the collective voice of sixteen Afro-Carib participants.[1] The findings that follow have the potential to produce transformative outcomes for nearly forty million people in the Caribbean, and beyond. Further, this research is offered to understand the relational phenomenon of creative practice and socioeconomic crisis in the Caribbean and all other developing nations reaching for sustainable growth. The project concludes with an epilogue that reflects my hope and compassion for the Afro-Carib culture.

Credibility of findings: establishing trustworthiness

In order to quench divergent findings through manipulated objectives, this project enhanced the conformability and credibility of the interpretations (Smith, Flowers and Larkin, 2009) by satisfying Lincoln and Guba's (1985) four step criteria for establishing trustworthiness in qualitative research—triangulation, direct quotation, awareness, and disconfirmation. *Triangulation* was achieved through the interpretations and perspectives of multiple researchers (Yardley, 2008).[2] Communicating directly with each of the researchers, via face-to-face conversations, email, Skype, or telephone, allowed independent and collective thought to elevate the credibility of the findings (Elliot, Fischer, & Rennie, 1999; Yardley, 2008).

The second step of *direct quotation* was satisfied through context and interpretation. Direct quotations from each participant was explicitly interpreted and coded through its respective context (Smith & Eatough, 2007). The direct quotes from the conversational interviews, which are the voice of the people, are the sole source of the outcomes for this project. Third, aware that my ontology and passion for the Afro-Carib culture could potentially influence the credibility of data collection, analysis, and findings, I fulfilled the *awareness* criteria through non-leading, open-ended questions throughout the conversational interviews (Table 5.4). The structure of each question limited my influence without compromising the integrity of the data and voice of the culture (Creswell, 2013). The final step of *disconfirmation* was achieved through the presentation of research at the University of Georgia.[3] Members of the UGA faculty, the Afro-Carib community, and the leadership of the UGA Afro-Carib Student Association were invited to attend, question, and challenge the research outcomes. Although there were a few oppositional statements from people who did not understand the depth of hardship for the Africans in the Caribbean, one UGA faculty member questioned the use of a structural term in the project. "Re-conditioned," is a phrase that was used to define the path to sustainable growth in the third lens of this research. As a result of the sound argument against the term, I revised the term assigned to the third theoretical lens in this project from "re-conditioned" to restoration.[4]

Findings: meanings, descriptions, and essences of lived experiences

The last stage of the analytic process identified synthesized theme units generated by the composite descriptions (Tables 6.1–6.7). The five theme units that follow were "synthesized to develop meaning and essences of the phenomenon" (Moustakas, 1994, p. 181). This section of the project is an expansion of understanding for each of the emergent themes that the conversational interviews generated. Each expansion identifies the respective theme,

Table 6.1 Synthesized theme unit 1

Evidentiary participant quotations for theme unit 1

- "Most of us recognize that our strength is in our oneness. We have a lot of people who come and go from St. John, but the West Indian culture seems to be resilient, true to itself. We are a family that has been through hard times and has to stayed together, even though we are still enduring hard times."—P15
- "We have a sense of belonging. All of my life I've had a sense of belonging to a family, something larger than just me. It's my security. No matter where I go or how far away I travel, I have security in knowing that I belong to the West Indian family in St. John."—P7
- "Everyone on this island is always just a phone call away. We are one big family. When we are in need, we always know that someone is there to help."—P12
- "Family is how we operate, we support each other, lift each other up."—P10
- "This island is one big family. It takes a village to raise kids and survive life. I feel I have a village that I trust and can depend on in St. John. Sometimes my immediate family is not available, but I can count on my St. John family to always be there for me."—P13
- "This is a cohesive community. No matter what, we work together. We know that we have to work together. There is a grassroots cohesion here that I have never witnessed like this island. We stick together to protect this island."—P14
- "I appreciate experiences of life more since we are one big family. As a big family in a community of love, we value each other."—P7

---

list evidentiary quotations that corroborate the theme, clarifies the content of the theme through an illustrated perspective, and recognizes theoretical positions in this project for added understanding to the theme.

Theme unit 1: a cohesive family unit

The Afro-Carib culture views itself as a cohesive family unit—strength and resilience are embedded in their oneness.

Corroborating meaning: juxtaposed to the historical progression of the region

Oneness for the Africans in the Caribbean is an ontological attribute. Césaire (1948) suggested that prior to the violent removal from Africa the culture collectivity, "built houses, governed empires, erected cities, cultivated fields, mined for metals, weaved cotton, and forged steel" (p. 7). He further stated, "Their customs were pleasing, built on unity, kindness, and respect for age. No coercion, only mutual assistance, the joy of living, a free acceptance of discipline" (Césaire, 1948, p. 7). Oneness for the Afro-Carib culture was not a product of enslavement; the unity among the people was a cultural attribute prior to imperialistic domination.

The 500 year history of the Africans in the Caribbean can be defined as survival through oneness (Rodney, 1972). The Afro-Caribs were violently displaced from Africa as one, shipped to the Caribbean as one, and enslaved by imperialistic nations as one. As one, the culture endured violence, managed oppression, lived through crisis, suffered through chaos, and resisted dependency (Zips, 2009). The oneness of the culture may not always be freely recognized due to "family" disagreements; however, no matter where one might travel throughout the world, there will be pockets of unified

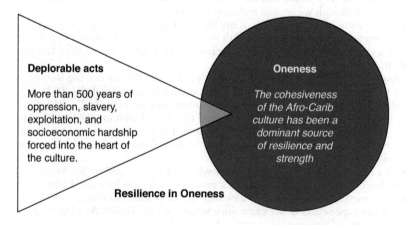

Figure 6.1 Illustrated synthesized theme unit 1: resilience in oneness.

Afro-Caribs celebrating the oneness and heritage of their culture. This position is comprehensively expanded and corroborated in the historical progression of the Caribbean in Chapter 3 and the section titled *Intentional creative practice is a source of resilience* in Chapter 4.

Synthesized theme confirmation

A peripheral objective of the conversational interviews was to identify a single term that defined the reality of Afro-Carib life (Table 5.4, question 2). Each participant was asked, "If you could sum up Afro-Carib life on St. John in one word, what would that word be?" The descriptive answers authenticate a stream of meaning in the findings (Table 6.6). Six of the participants described life in the Caribbean as a variant of hard, while ten participants identified Afro-Carib life as a variant of connectedness.

Theme unit 2: socioeconomic crisis is deconstructing a sense of place

Socioeconomic crisis is deconstructing a sense of place for the Afro-Carib people, which contributes to the breakdown of solidarity in the culture and facilitates migration out of the region.

Corroborating meaning: juxtaposing the Afro-Carib voice to the historical progression and theoretical analysis

Erisman (2003) suggested, "poverty and unemployment fuel migration, and the Caribbean has the highest percentage of migrants of any world region" (p. 173). The scope of Afro-Carib migration is disclosed in Kristen McCabe's

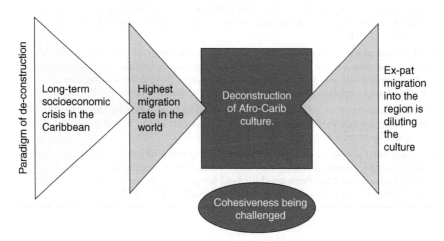

Figure 6.2 Illustrated synthesized theme unit 2: paradigm of deconstruction.

Table 6.2 Synthesized theme unit 2

Evidentiary participant quotations for theme unit 2

- "My generation is leaving this island by the droves since they see no hope or potential for opportunities here on St. John."—P15
- "The island is on the verge of falling apart! The cost of living. Cost of doing business. It is absolutely a crisis! Our culture is killing itself with so many bad economic decisions. All my friends are leaving."—P16
- "I thought my friends and I would be together for many years to come, but most of them left. Kids used to leave after high school to go to college, but now kids are leaving in grade school and do not return. The economic situation makes it difficult to stay and even more difficult to return."—P15
- "It's hard. It's hard all the time. My parents talk about it a lot. At home, it is the same as school. We have problems, our water doesn't work sometimes, and food is so expensive that we can't always get what we need. It's the reason why so many people are leaving. Yes, it is a crisis."—P3
- "The new people take our houses. Soon there will not be any West Indians living on St. John."—P4
- "My son is the class president of his 5th grade. He announced to me several nights ago that when he reaches the 8th grade, we are relocating to the states for "opportunities." The economic situation has kept the territory from creating opportunities. Adults know it, kids know it."—P10
- "Most West Indians have to work two or three jobs just to survive. We are selling lands that have been in our families for generations to survive. Since most of the new owners are not West Indians, our customs and traditions are being effected negativity. West Indians are leaving everyday. We are losing our culture."—P12
- "It's expensive on St. John. The supplies, needs, food, bills and other stuff are expensive. Yes, I think it's a crisis because everything is expensive. It everything wasn't so expensive people would not be leaving."—P1
- The economy is causing us to lose our best-educated people. We are losing homegrown people. In my school, the number of native St. Johnian students is dwindling fast. Families are moving away at greater numbers than I can ever remember."—P7
- "The cost of living is out of control. Politics are forcing our people to leave. It's the reason why we are losing people. We are giving unqualified people positions of power just because they worked on a campaign. People are leaving due to political appointments. As a result, we are losing quality people."—P9
- "Things continue to get worse. The cost of living is going up by the year, and the wages are not increasing to match it. That is part of the reason why a lot of people I went to school leave do not return."—P11
- "Many local people have a hard time purchasing items of need. I would say that the economic situation is most definitely a crisis that is getting worse. So many West Indians that have been on this island for generations are having to leave the island because they cannot afford to stay. It's really sad."—P12

(2015) report from The Migration Policy Institute. Based on McCabe's findings, over 25% of Caribbean born people now live abroad, compared to 1.2% of Americans who live abroad and 0.75% of Brazilians who live abroad (Focus-Migration, 2016). High migration rates suggest that a sense of self, sense of place, and realized potential has been destabilized (Runco, 2014), which defines the long-term socioeconomic crisis in the Caribbean (Girvan, 2011)

Walcott (2000) further suggested that Afro-Caribs migrate for opportunity and mobility. Based on Walcott's (2000) assessment, it seems plausible that the high rate of Afro-Carib migration could be driven by a creative deficit in transportation and opportunity, both indicators of socioeconomic crisis (Girvan, 2002). The International Monetary Fund (2005) concluded that the Caribbean has the highest rate of migration of any region in the world; 40% of its labor force has migrated in the last decade (International Monetary Fund, 2012). Some island nations "have lost up to 70% of their work force with more than 12 years of schooling, which is the highest rate of migration in the world" (International Monetary Fund, 2005). Based on the assessments of Girvan (2002), Runco (2014), Walcott (2000), and the data from the International Monetary Fund (2005), a destabilized sense of place for the Africans in the Caribbean has resulted in socioeconomic crisis.

The historical progression of the region corroborates this position that Afro-Caribs migrate due to socioeconomic crisis. An example is the collective decisions in the development period (see Chapter 3). The political and economic decisions fortified dependency and created high levels of poverty, which in turn stimulated a migration crisis that affects the current reality of life in the region.[5] The analyses of all five historical periods in the Caribbean reveal meaning that produces the highest migration rate in the world.

Table 6.3 Synthesized theme confirmation

SPEC question (Table 6.1)	Variants of hardship	Variants of family
If you could sum up Afro-Carib life on St. John in one word, what would that word be?	Change – P1 Tough – P2 Hard – P4 Behind – P7 Lost – P9 Stagnate – P8	Love – P3 Beautiful – P5 Beautiful – P6 Family – P10 Home – P11 Paradise – P12 Family – P13 Cohesive – P14 Family – P15 Family – P16

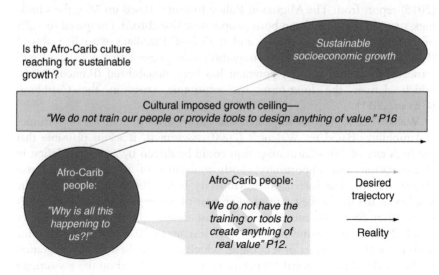

Figure 6.3 Illustrated synthesized theme unit 3: sustainable growth.

Theme unit 3: individual and cultural growth is inhibited

Individual and cultural growth is inhibited by inadequate access to instruction, tools, and environments, which prohibit culturally exclusive innovation.

Corroborating meaning: juxtaposing the Afro-Carib voice to the historical progression and theoretical analysis

The historical progression of the region (Chapter 3) suggests that people enslaved through colonial oppression were conditioned to "not use their minds, invent things, create institutions of history, imagine, produce anything of value, or practice the arts of civilization" (Smith, 1999, p. 25). The imperialistic agenda further included a suppression of cognitive processes that included creative practice, imagination, and the art of civilization (Olwig, 1985; Zips, 2009). Accomplishing these objectives required the imperialistic oppressors to remove environments, tools, and instruction that facilitated creative innovation. The strategic act denied access to the essential components of growth, while concurrently prohibiting the Afro-Carib people from realizing their potential and independence.

The theoretical analysis of the region (Chapter 4) argues that creative practice specifically refers to the type of activity within the environment—i.e., shaping and re-shaping a conceptual idea into an implemented reality through the access of tools, facilities, and instruction (Runco, 2014). De Bono (1992) suggests that creativity is a skill that must be practiced and nurtured to produce effective outcomes. Thus, in order to move an individual or culture beyond the status quo, original ideas must be implemented and deemed

Table 6.4 Synthesized theme unit 3

Evidentiary participant quotations for theme unit 3

- "We do not have the training or tools to create anything of real value. Do we have the capacity? Absolutely!" —P12
- "I do not feel most of the culture is provided with tools to make a real change for the overall culture." —P14
- "We don't train our people or provide them with the tools to design anything of value." —P16
- "This is so frustrating to me. This year we were so excited when we started a cooking class at school. The first day the teacher tells us all about what we are going to learn to cook. The second day she said we are going to learn how to measure ingredients until the stoves are repaired. Two weeks later, she tells that class that the stoves are still not repaired, so we are to go onto the field and play. It's November and we are still going to the field to play during that period." —P1
- "We had that class, but the teacher retired and they don't teach it any longer. Most of us loved that class because it taught us a lot of stuff, We did sewing, crochet, made pillows, mats, a whole lot of stuff. I'm disappointed that class is gone, I liked that class." —P3
- "I do not feel I have the proper tools to be creative in the Virgin Islands." —P3
- "School did not prepare for life or business and I do not believe our kids are being prepared to face a financial life. Life here is hard and we need to be prepared to handle hard issues related to our finances. I do not believe we are prepared." —P16
- "I know that our schools operate on the bare minimum, which cheats our kids out of opportunities. Our kids do not get opportunities because we are so far behind. There are real reasons why we are behind. Decades of bad economic decisions from our government have left us and our schools behind." —P14
- "We are not giving our culture a chance. We are not preparing kids for life. It seems we are only consumed with survival." —P14
- "We always talk about home economics and music, but we never have those classes. Sad." —P13
- "The only school supplies we have to make things are magnets and paper clips." —P13
- "I believe we have been limited in what we do, we are always stuck, stuck, stuck." —P12 "We don't have enough money to fix things at school, to make things right." —P5
- "I do think that the kids think they can change things, but maybe they have not been fully expose to the dysfunction in the government. I hope we can find some way for this generation of kids to change things for the good." —P7
- "Our leadership is a group of people who have not encouraged us to grow as individuals or as territory." —P9 •
- "Tools are not provided here. The tools come with the people. If we don't have the teachers who have an open mind to instruct in a creative way, it doesn't matter if you have the tools. You can have the most resources in the world, but if you do not have the leadership there to foster creativity and listen to kids, we will always be behind." —P1
- "We used to have wood working classes and cooking classes in school, but they stopped teaching those subjects many years ago." —P12
- "I believe it is unrealistic for me create something that would change life on St John." —P3
- "I do not feel I have the proper tools to be creative. I like to create arts and crafts, sometimes I want to build a solar car, but I do not have the tools. I like to build a go-cart, or a rocket, soccer net, but I don't have the tools to build any of that. I believe it's realistic that I could create something to change life for West Indians on St. John. I believe that anyone has the power to do anything, but you have to have the right tools." —P2

effective through a process of intentional creative practice. However, if access to environments, tools, and instruction are denied, the culture is prohibited from realizing their potential and sustainable growth.

Theme unit 4: the cultural value of creativity

The Afro-Carib creative influence has been reduced to non-sustainable items.

Corroborating meaning: juxtaposing the Afro-Carib voice to the historical progression and theoretical analysis

Historically, the value of unleashed potential has yet to be realized for the Africans in the Caribbean. Eric Williams, Trinidad and Tobago's first Prime Minister proposed, "The entire Caribbean Basin could hold a dignified global position if the African culture would realize its potential" (1993, p. 148). Based on the historical record and the present reality of crisis, Grugel (1995) suggests that long term socioeconomic crisis in the Caribbean prevents the culture from realizing their potential. He argues that

> [a] series of crises in the Caribbean prevents the people of the region from realizing their potential. Unless these problems are addressed, the region will continue to face deepening poverty for most of the

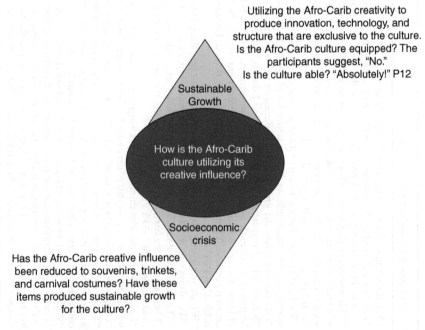

Figure 6.4 Illustrated synthesized theme unit 4: creativity.

Table 6.5 Synthesized theme unit 4

Evidentiary participant quotations for theme unit 4

- "I am someone who is trapped in a body to create, but was not taught to create. How am I supposed to make it happen? This system in the Virgin Islands is to go to school, graduate and work for the government until its time to retire. That is why my mother left. She had no opportunity to be creative in the Virgin Islands. She felt she was cheating herself by remaining here."—P9
- "Creativity? None, none, none! No classes that allowed me or taught me to be creative."—P10
- "I have not seen anyone paint or invent anything on St John."—P4
- "I did not do many projects in school when I was growing up, I don't remember the opportunity to be creative inside of my classes."—P11
- "There is nothing for the kids in arts. Kid's love programs of creativity, we just don't have any. One of the reasons: People do not take us seriously when it comes to education. The federal government has different criteria for us. We have yet to receive our federal funding for this school year. Every time we submit the application, it comes back with more criteria. Life in this territory has become about survival"—P10
- "The only creativity I see on St. John is coconut shells made into all types of containers, candles, and birdhouses. I really cannot think of any consistent creativity that comes from the West Indian family."—P7
- "The only creativity I see on the island is carnival, costumes, floats, arts and crafts at the ruins in Anaberg. But creativity seems to be event driven. I do not see a lot of creativity unless it is for an event."—P11
- "I believe creativity is my gift. Recently, I began to ask students about their gifts, what are you gifted at doing? The answers broke my heart, kids lowered their heads, the majority did not have an answer."—P10
- "I mean there are silly little crafts that some people sell on the side of the road, but beyond that, I cannot think of any creative expressions."—P16
- "The mentality of life here is still survival, from one day to the next. We do not invest in creative people."—P16
- "They use beads and marbles to create jewelry and other types of artwork. I just wished that type of creativity was used in the schools."—P13
- "The only thing creative think I see people doing on the island is making boots and costumes for Carnival."—P4

population, *whatever* the macroeconomic situation, and thus potential political instability.

(Grugel, 1995, p. 233)

Due to the length and weight of the socioeconomic crisis, the culture has seemingly surrendered its potential for achievement, which reduces life to daily decisions of survival. Recognizing the need to transform their identity, Shepherd (2011) suggested that an awakened consciousness and purpose for the Africans in the Caribbean would only come through realized *potential*. Grugel (1995), Williams (1993), and Shepherd (2011) have all suggested that regardless of the political or economic structures, crisis will continue to abound unless individuals can move past a survivalist mentality by realizing their full *potential*.

Theoretically, Runco (2014) suggests, "political conditions influence the expression of creativity and the fulfillment of creative potential" (p. 303). However, creative practice as a key component of political reform or social change has been historically marginalized. Thus, the reason that political structures and/or economic policies have not proved to be viable solutions to the socioeconomic crisis in the Caribbean is their failure to prioritize the culture's full *potential*. The Africans in the Caribbean cannot move beyond their current status to establish a true identity based solely on political structures or economic policies. When Runco (2014) spoke of unrealized potential, he also argued that "creating a sense of self" is imperative for independence and sustainable development (p. 219). Based on Runco's (2014) position, true identity is recognized when potential is realized; realized potential is a product of intentional environments of creative practice.

Based on the stated positions, elevating the priority of creative practice in political policy has the potential to diffuse the socioeconomic crisis, which would facilitate independence and autonomy. Regarding the cultures of the Caribbean, the pathway to sustainable growth (Figure 4.3) requires political leaders to intentionally guide creative practice to the center of national policy. This project includes an expansive analysis of *potential* in the section titled *Unburying cultural expression: Transforming identity by unleashing potential*. The expansion and its conceivable outcomes are located in Chapter 4.

Theme unit 5: creativity is innate and essential

The Afro-Carib people recognize that creativity is an innate cultural attribute and essential for a future of sustainable growth.

Corroborating meaning: creative practice is innate and essential

The final theme unit utilizes a synthesized textural and structural analysis generated in a word cloud to illustrate the voice of the Afro-Carib culture (Figure 6.6). The word cloud was generated by NVivo 10 qualitative research

Table 6.6 Synthesized theme unit 5

Evidentiary participant quotations for theme unit 5

- "Creativity is the mother child of our culture. Creativity plays a central role in our culture, in the past, present, and future. Our forefathers used creativity to grow their African cultures, and then used their creativity to survive. Why can't we? Our foundation as a culture is creativity."—P7
- "It is simple, without creativity we don't own it and we will not grow."—P16
- "Our culture starts with creativity."—P11
- "We must have creative leaders to get us out of our problems. If leaders aren't willing to be creative, we will never get out of the problems. But I see us making the same bad decisions over and over again."—P7
- I believe creativity is at the center of our culture. I believe creativity is a fundamental step. We as a collective culture see it in other cultures. Unfortunately, I think when we see it, we try to make it work here, which does not work since we are not prepared or have the tools."—P15
- "I believe a lack of creativity has negativity influenced and influences our economy. I believe that once our kids have the freedom and opportunity to create more things that our economy will be positivity affected."—P13
- "We have to use creativity to build our island and culture. Without it, we remain stuck in the past."—P12
- "Creativity is the only way we can move forward. In order to make products that the world will want to purchase, we have to gain some clarity, feel our culture, and embrace our culture first. I admit, it feels naïve or weird to try to be something that we are not. We were set up to be a resource center for the US population, but that is not our culture. To move forward as a culture, we have to be true to who we are as a culture."—P9
- "Creativity has a direct impact on revenue and purpose. We don't promote creativity, so it negatively impacts our revenue and advancement. Creativity is essential to our survival."—P10

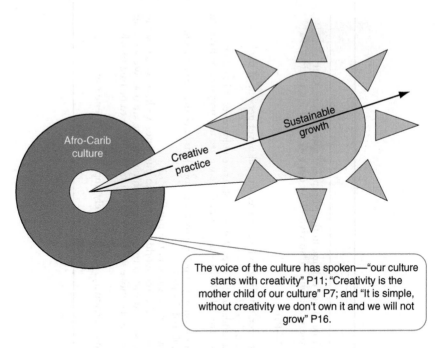

Figure 6.5 Illustrated synthesized theme unit 5: creative practice.

software in the final stage of the synthesized analysis. The illustration correlates the weight and frequency of the participant's words to the themes generated from the analysis.

Pessimistic positions suggests that word clouds distort reality. An example
would be, "a word cloud is like reading tealeaves at the bottom of a cup, what's
left is a shoddy visualization that fails all the principles of reality" (Harris, 2011,
p. 1). However, based on the findings in this project, the word cloud seems to
accurately depict the reality of life for the Afro-Carib people (Figure 6.6).

Recognizing that the word cloud illustrates the texture, priorities, and
concerns of the Afro-Carib "people," it further accentuates the depth of the
relationship between creativity and the Afro-Carib people. The word cloud
distinguishes the depth of the relationship through two approaches; the most
obvious is the visual element that insinuates weight and meaning through the
size of the term. Second, the assignment of synthesized order, which is pre-
dicated on the weight and meanings of the Afro-Carib voice (Table 6.7).

The outcomes of the synthesized weight and meanings of the Afro-Carib
voice suggests that the "people" are "thinking" about the hardship of life and
the role that "creativity" plays in the development of their "culture, family,
and island." The "people believe" they are capable of sustainable growth;
however, they do not believe their "schools" are equipping or preparing the
"people" for initiatives required for sustainable growth. Therefore, it seems

Figure 6.6 Word cloud: synthesized meaning for the Afro-Carib culture.

Table 6.7 Synthesized words of weight and meaning

Terms	Weight	Significance
People	1	The highest priority of the culture is the wellbeing of the "people."
Think	2	The culture as a whole "thinks" about the struggle and future.
Creative	3	The culture recognizes their "creative" ontology.
School	4	The culture suggests they have not been prepared for growth in "school."
Believe	5	The culture "believes" they are capable of producing sustainable growth.
Creativity	6	Due to a lack of tools and instruction—culture not equipped for "creativity."
Culture	7	The Afro-Carib people remain passionate and faithful to their "culture."
Island	8	The "island" is home, no matter the migration destination.
Life	9	The growth and quality of "life" is a troublesome reality for the culture.
Family	10	The Afro-Carib culture is one large "family."

Note
Word cloud terms are in descending order based on synthesized weight.

plausible to suggest that the "people" are forced to migrate outside the region for instruction, tools, and creative environments to realize their fullest potential. Based on that premise, I am suggesting that an intentional strategy to facilitate open access environments of creativity, procure instruction, and provide tools, would slow migration, restore the suppressed identity, elevate a sense of self, and allow potential to be realized—all central components in the socioeconomic crisis.

Concluding remarks

All four components in this project suggest a similar outcome for the studied phenomenon; a bi-directional relationship exists between creative practice and socioeconomic crisis in the Caribbean.[6] My observations as an participant in Caribbean life, historical progression of the region, theoretical analysis, and the voice of the people, all indicate that active and intentional creative practice is directly correlated with socioeconomic health in the Caribbean. Thus, cultural restoration and sustainable growth for the cultures in the Caribbean are dependent on strategic and intentional environments of creative practice.[7]

The findings in this project substantiate that the access to environments, instruction, and tools of creative practice are contingencies for sustainable socioeconomic growth (Runco, 2014). When referencing the Africans in the Caribbean, Naipaul (1969), Memmi (1956), Olwig (1985), and Rodney (1972) suggest that free and open access to creative practice was strategically suppressed to ensure that the Caribbean would remain underdeveloped. Thus, based on comprehensive analysis in this project, intentionally suppressed environments of creative practice have perpetuated the long-term socioeconomic crisis in the Caribbean.

The cultures of the Caribbean are challenged with a decision that will influence many generations to come—accept the dysfunctional socio-economic reality as status quo or strategically facilitate open access to environments of creative practice. As historically confirmed in the region, the dysfunctional status quo has far reaching implications—more non-sustainable development, longer-term socioeconomic crisis, unrealized cultural potential, and higher migration rates. However, developing and facilitating open access to environments of creative practice provides a viable pathway to sustainable growth for all cultures in the Caribbean.

This project provides a clear and intentional path for a restored cultural identity, true independence, and sustainable growth for the Caribbean cultures. The path is inclusive of an educational process that should sustain the culture—one that grants open access to environments of creative practice, provides the essential tools, and secures the foremost instruction. As Participant 7 in this project astutely articulated;

> Creativity is the mother child of our culture. Creativity plays a central role in our culture, in the past, present, and future. Our forefathers used

creativity to grow their African cultures, and then used their creativity to survive. Why can't we? Our foundation as a culture is creativity.

(Participant 7)

If the foundation of the culture is void of an essential component, then it seems plausible to suggest that the structure built on the foundation will remain unstable and teetering on the precipice of collapse. Therefore, based on the findings of this project, it seems imperative that institutions of education, governments, corporations, houses of worship, and all concerned residents in the Caribbean collectively and intentionally establish environments of creative practice to ensure independence and sustainable economic growth for generations to come.

My expanded reality

Nearly twenty years of residency in the Caribbean solidified my perspective of the reality of life in the region—or so I thought. Although I achieved what I set out to accomplish in this project—which was to comprehensively identify "why" long-term socioeconomic crisis in the Caribbean continues to create a debilitating hardship for its residents—the findings in this project expanded my perspective of reality for the Afro-Carib culture. The *intentionality* of oppression, motivations of migration, suppression of the Afro-Carib voice, and an illuminated path to sustainable growth provided a lens of understanding that my twenty-year positionality unknowingly excluded. An analysis of each of these realities challenged me to reconstitute my path of participation in the restoration process of the Caribbean cultures. The following segments are an expansion of how the analysis and findings in this project expanded my perspective of life in the Caribbean.

Troubled by intentionality

Throughout my residency in the Caribbean, I begrudgingly observed friends, acquaintances, and strangers from outside the region freely express their judgments and disdain for the Afro-Carib culture. The prevailing position seemed to be a distorted stereotypical assessment that defined the culture as, "lazy, corrupt, and dope smoking Rastafarians." Many of those false judgments digressed to a point of ineptness, which surmised: "the Afro-Carib people will never rise above their current dysfunctional state." Although I relentlessly and passionately refuted the false judgments, internally I struggled with the reality of my first-hand observations—Why would an angry mob pilfer the contents of a man's car as he lay dead against the steering wheel? Why would a ten-year old boy attempt to rob me at knifepoint standing in the front door of Burger King? Why would an angry Rastafarian yell death threats at me for one year? Why would five thieves hold my colleague and I at gunpoint?[8]

Emanating from the core of my struggle was a confounding reality; "why" does a culture rooted in "paradise," whose lifestyle remains a source of envy for many impressionable minds around the world, feel the need to participate in cold, calculating, and deplorable behavior? Extensively answering the confounding reality was a motivation for this project—"There must be a reason 'why' crisis and chaos seem to be a prevailing reality within the Caribbean cultures." The comprehensive analysis and findings in this project clarified my confusion and identified *intentional* suppression as the foremost source of anger and suffering in the Caribbean. In order for the imperialistic nations to secure a profit, *intentional* acts of suppression with outcomes of deplorable hardship had to be embedded into the foundation of the culture. Beginning the day that Columbus arrived in the Caribbean in 1492, the region was viewed as a strategic profit center.[9] Tragically, securing a profit required *intentional* acts of suppression that continue to impede the Caribbean cultures more than 500 years later.

Further clarifying my assessment of reality in the Caribbean was my lengthy list of questions that began with "why," such as—"Why are all these things happening in the Caribbean?"[10] "Why is the crime rate in the Caribbean the highest of any region in the world?" "Why is socioeconomic hardship an ever-present reality?" "Why is the migration rate in the region the highest in the world?" "Why is authentic innovation in the Caribbean limited?" "Why are there only small increments of sustainable growth in the Caribbean?" The historical and theoretical findings in this project suggest each of these questions has *intentional* suppression in their origin.

Ironically, identifying the source of "why" transformed my internal struggle to a state of restless anger—my struggle was no longer defined solely by the reality of long-term hardship for the Afro-Carib culture, my anger was inflamed by the substance and debilitating influence of *intentionality*. For several months the findings of *intentional* suppression agitated my emotions and disrupted my sleep. The restless anger prompted to me to evaluate my educational leadership in the region and strategically assess my level of effectiveness through a lens of sustainable growth.

Having served in educational leadership positions in the Caribbean for nearly two decades allowed me to establish intimate relationships and a passionate affection for the Afro-Carib culture on Jamaica, British Virgin Islands, and the U.S. Virgin Islands. However, due to the realized effects of *intentional* suppression, my perspective and focus were altered from a local method of education to a region-wide process of cultural restoration. No longer could my sphere of participation be confined to a few islands, my transformed state of perspective motivated me to broaden my lens of participation by developing an initiative of cultural restoration through sustainable growth for forty million people throughout the Caribbean home.[11]

Motivated to migrate from "paradise"

Migration from the Caribbean is a confounding reality. While the majority of the world seems to view the Caribbean through a lens of "paradise," the region has maintained the highest migration rate of any region in the world for four consecutive decades.[12] The lens of "paradise" seems to suggest, "go to the Caribbean at all costs," yet the migration rate seems to indicate, "escape the Caribbean at all costs." Migration from the region remains a debilitating phenomenon that produces outcomes of cultural dysfunction and long-term socioeconomic crisis in the region.[13]

As an observer, employer, colleague, and friend of many in the Caribbean, migration is an unavoidable reality. The subject is a perpetual conversation at all levels of the culture and requires strategic management of structures and emotions. The predominant justification for migration that I witnessed from employees, colleagues, and friends was, "I must leave the island for opportunities of personal growth." However, the findings of this project suggest that the desire for "opportunities for personal growth" is a residual effect of the intentional suppression of a sense of self, place, and potential. The suppression of each of those respective components was central to the cultural conditioning strategy carried out by the imperialistic nations.[14] Embedded within the act of relocating from the Caribbean, the cultures seem to be communicating an explicit message, "I matter, my life matters, and my future matters."

Voice with feet

Although the prevailing desire for migration from the Caribbean seems to be *personal growth*, the findings in this project suggest that the factors that define personal growth are the true catalysts of departure—a sense of self, place, and realized potential constitute *personal growth*. Further, the rate of migration from the Caribbean suggests that the people view the restoration of self, place, and realized potential as matters of intentional suppression, which implies that people have lost hope in cultural restoration on their respective islands. Based on my observations and the voice of the participants in this project, the people are voicing their desire for intentional restoration with their feet. Their collective action seems to be saying, "We want a restored sense of self, place, and realized potential; if we cannot get it here, we will relocate to a place that will freely allow us to achieve our objectives of personal growth."[15]

This project identified a portal of understanding regarding migration from the Caribbean—if the voice of the people is suppressed, then migration flourishes. The analysis of the historical progression of the Caribbean reveals a profound lesson regarding the voice of the people—voice can only be suppressed for a segment of time before one of two realities emerge—revolt or departure—both of which are current realities in the Caribbean. Thus, the outcomes of this project clarified for me, as the investigator, that migration from the Caribbean is the result of a suppressed *voice* that learned to walk.

Creative practice—transforming "why" to "how"

The migration phenomenon in the Caribbean is embedded with a troubling component—the people do not want to leave the region.[16] The decision for Caribbean people to relocate from their home islands is not related to "island fever" nor flippant wanderlust; the decision to relocate from family, heritage, and culture is an excruciating process of tearing away. Irrespective of the island nation, the Caribbean cultures are enormously patriotic to their home islands. The people are colorfully proud of their respective Caribbean heritage and openly celebrate their unique identity among other Caribbean nationals. As the participants in this project revealed, the individuals that comprise an island culture view their respective islands as one large family.[17] Therefore, the decision to migrate out of the region exposes an extinguished hope for accessing opportunities of personal growth on their home islands. Based on the findings in this project, if a sense of self, place, and unrealized potential are not culturally prioritized, then people legitimately conclude that there is minimal hope for personal growth.[18]

Through the historical progression, theoretical analysis, and the voice of the people; this project expanded on the outcomes related to the relationship between environments of personal growth and socioeconomic crisis.[19] In order for me to effectively develop a personal response of "how" to respectfully participate in dismantling the socioeconomic hardship, I comprehensively analyzed the outcomes in this project to develop a path of sustainable growth for the cultures of the Caribbean. Utilizing Capra's (2002) model of sustainable growth for all living organisms, my cultural restoration response was not developed on the current socioeconomic realities in the Caribbean, but developed through a two-step vertical inquiry. First, I identified the origins of "why" socioeconomic crisis exists in the Caribbean. Second, I sought to diffuse the dysfunctional influences of the past with sustainable life giving components for the future.

The following is a bulleted review of "why" long-term socioeconomic crisis exists in the Caribbean. Each represents a point of dysfunctional influence that I utilized to develop my response of sustainable growth.

1   The initial conditions of the region were embedded crisis and chaos.
2   Intentional and long-term cultural conditioning by imperialistic nations.
3   Suppressed voice for over 500 years.
4   Suppressed sense of self and place.
5   Unrealized and suppressed potential.
6   Limited access to environments of creative practice, instruction, and tools.
7   Indiscernible strategy for cultural restoration.

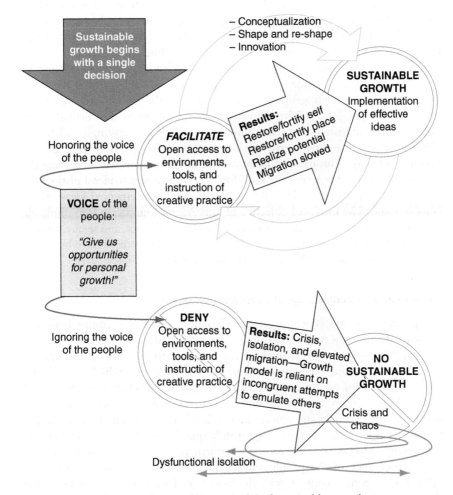

Figure 6.7 The decision: the *create2elevate* model of sustainable growth.

Having identified the factors of "why" long-term socioeconomic crisis exists in the region, the next step in my restoration progression utilizes the findings in this project to develop "how" I can participate in securing a pathway of sustainable growth for the cultures in the Caribbean.

Participating in restoration—create2elevate

Respective to this project, cultural restoration is defined as a strategic and intentional transformation from socioeconomic crisis to sustainable growth. Thus, I developed the *create2elevate* foundation to specifically dismantle socio-economic crisis, slow migration, and facilitate sustainable growth by restoring a sense of self, place, and realized potential to the individuals of the Caribbean cultures. Effectively developing and implementing the *create2elevate* foundation, which is a derivative of this project, is "how" I respectively request to participate in the intentional restoration of the Caribbean cultures.

The *create2elevate* foundation recognizes that individuals, cultures, and/or corporations can all be defined as living organisms. Sustainable growth for every living organism is contingent upon two attributes, the capacity to create and regenerate (Capra, 2002). When those capacities are suppressed or denied; crisis, isolation, and ultimately death are imminent realities. Contrastingly, when the capacities to create and regenerate are intentionally facilitated, sustainable growth becomes a reality. Through the facilitation of environments that accentuate the creative insights of the respective workforce, *create2elevate* provides a platform of voice that elevates the whole of the culture through implemented ideas of sustainable value. The missional objective of *create2elevate* foundation is to dismantle socioeconomic crisis, slow the migration of innovative talent, and secure sustainable growth through implemented innovation derived from those who know the needs and nuances of the culture and/or organization (Figure 6.7).[20]

Confirmation of authenticity: the decision to respond

My positionality and affection for the Caribbean cultures is comprehensively acknowledged in this project. Thus, the authenticity of my affection for the cultures will be judged and defined by my response to the findings. Further, I recognize that a single decision will define the outcome, which is to either allow the findings to remain a theoretical work or develop an implemented reality. A decision to confine the work to a theoretical conversation is to deny the voice of the people and ignore the depth of socioeconomic hardship in the Caribbean. The decision would legitimately qualify my efforts in this project as self-serving. However, a decision to implement a transformational response honors the voice of the people and validates my authentic affection for the culture. One path is content with the long-term hardship in the region while the other seeks sustainable growth for forty million people in the Caribbean. I am choosing respectful restoration, what about you? I conclude this comprehensive project with a personal letter to all people in the Caribbean.

> *12 June 2016*
> *To all political leaders, corporate directors, innovative entrepreneurs, and all people from the Caribbean who desire to dismantle socioeconomic crisis and secure a future of sustainable growth.*
>
> *Good day. As a nearly twenty-year resident in the region, I have shared in your hardship, understand your bitterness, and passionately desire a self-sustaining future for you. My response to the reality illuminated in this project is to respectfully request your guidance and collaboration in implementing the create2elevate foundation throughout the Caribbean. Therefore, I am seeking face-to-face meetings with all political, corporate, and educational leaders throughout the region to*

discuss the dismantling of socioeconomic crisis and the development of true inde-pendence for the generations to come.

In the same light that the findings in this project challenged me to reconstitute my sphere of participation in cultural restoration, I emphatically request that all people from the Caribbean substantiate your authentic love for your culture by col-lectively participating in the socioeconomic restoration of your culture. Now is the time to refrain from blame, reject the status quo of socioeconomic crisis, and secure a future of sustainable growth for your culture.

The decision to reach for cultural restoration rests with you and your resolute willingness to rise above the long-term hardship that has debilitated your culture for over 500 years. Are you willing to engage, shape, and implement culturally derived ideas that have affluent value for your future generations? The findings in this project suggest that opportunity to end socioeconomic crisis and realize sustain-able growth exists for all, including you. I will close my plea for collective collabo-ration with a Jamaican phrase that has motivated many oppressed people in the Caribbean to resist the conditions in the present by clearing the path for genera-tions to come—"Man nu dead, nu call dem deh puppy!" Translation: Don't underestimate the people!

Have a creative day.

In the highest respect with one love,
Kent J. Wessinger, Ph.D.

Future research

Although the findings of this project develop an understanding of the rela-tionship between creative practice and socioeconomic crisis in the Caribbean, future research should develop methods and priorities for implementing spe-cific components of creative practice within the Caribbean cultures. The methods and priorities should not be limited to the following, but inclusive of curriculum of creative practice for all school-aged children, methods of efficacy for instruction, continuums through higher education, forms of meas-urement, collective objectives for government leadership, departments of education, institutions of higher learning, and community organizations. Last, future research should prioritize the development and outcomes of respectful collaboration between island nations and developed countries—the collabora-tion should be void of colonial motivations and structures. The Afro-Carib culture is too volatile and essential to the global community to refrain from further research.

Epilogue

When I relocated to rural Jamaica in 1994 to become the headmaster of the Institute of the Caribbean, I had no idea that the Afro-Carib culture and its plight would become my lifelong passion. After residing in the region for nearly two decades, the culture transformed my understanding of relationship, priority, and privilege. Today, I am honored that my most cherished friendships are in the islands, that all three of my children call the Caribbean "home," and that my identity is steeped in the Afro-Carib culture. Although I remained burdened by the longstanding hardship for the culture, I am intentionally committed to participant in ventures of sustainable growth for my beloved friends in the Caribbean. Peace out mi boi—One love!

Notes

1 This chapter contains two designations for the Africans living in the Caribbean—Afro-Caribs and West Indians. Refer to Glossary A.
2 Fitzroy Beckford, PhD; Mark Runco, PhD; Pramod Parajuli, PhD.
3 The research presentation, entitled, "Why is all this happening in 'Paradise?'—The relationship between creative practice and socioeconomic crisis the Caribbean," was held in the Zell Miller Learning Center on the University of Georgia campus on April 8, 2016.
4 In Chapter 4, Lens III is titled *Strength through restoration—intentional creative practice*.
5 Refer to the section titled *Developmental period (1955–1982): forfeited independence* (Chapter 3) for detailed expansion on the position.
6 Respective to this project, *creativity* is defined as, "Vital originality balanced with fit and appropriateness" (Runco, 1988, p. 4); whereas, *practice* is defined as engaging, shaping, and implementing original ideas that are deemed effective through a process.
7 Respective to this project, cultural restoration is defined as a strategic and intentional transformation from socioeconomic crisis to sustainable growth—a process of restoring a sense of self, place, and realized potential to the individuals in the cultures of the Caribbean.
8 Each of the events is expanded in Chapter 2.
9 "Columbus stated, 'I could conquer the whole of them with fifty men and govern them as I pleased'" (as cited in Columbus & Tosconelli, 2010, p. 41). Higman (2011), a historian who has comprehensively analyzed the Caribbean, offers an interpretation of Columbus's remarks: "He immediately saw them as potentially well fitted for labour" (p. 60). "The horrific events that define Caribbean Colonialism seemed to have been birthed the moment that Columbus arrived" (Wessinger, 2015, p. 42).
10 Intentionality: see Chapter 4.
11 create2elevate—the objectives of the foundation are located at create2elevate.com and in the section of this chapter titled *Participating in restoration*.
12 Chapter 3.
13 Chapter 3 and Chapter 4.
14 Chapter 3 and Chapter 4.
15 Migrants from the Caribbean overwhelmingly migrate to one of three geographical locations; United States, Canada, or Western Europe (see Chapter 3).
16 The participants interviewed for this project indicated that leaving the region is not their desired outcome for life (see Chapter 6).
17 *Chapter* 6.
18 Chapter 4.
19 *Personal growth* is an outcome of intentionally implemented environments of creative practice.
20 Further information related to the *create2elevate* foundation can be found at create2elevate.com or kentjwessinger.com

References

Capra, F. (2002). *The hidden connections: Integrating the biological, cognitive, and social dimensions of life into a science of sustainability.* New York, NY: Doubleday.

Capra, F., & Luisi, P. (2014). *The systems view of life: A unifying vision.* Cambridge: Cambridge Press.

Césaire, A. (1948). *Discourse on colonialism.* New York, NY: Monthly Review Press.

Creswell, J. (2007). *Qualitative inquiry & research design: Choosing among five approaches.* London: Sage Publications.

Creswell, J. (2013). *Qualitative inquiry & research design: Choosing among five approaches* (2nd ed.). London: Sage Publications.

de Bono, E. (1992). *Opportunities.* Westminster: Penguin Books.

Elliot, R., Fischer, C. T., & Rennie, D. L. (1999). Evolving guidelines for publication of qualitative research studies in psychology and related fields. *British Journal of Clinical Psychology,* 38: 215–229. DOI:10.1348/014466599162782.

Erisman, M. (2003). International relations. In R. Hillman, & T. D'Agostino (Eds), *Understanding the Contemporary Caribbean.* Boulder, CO: Lynne Rienner, pp. 161–187.

Focus-Migration (2016, January). Retrieved from www.focus-migration.hwwi.de

Girvan, N. (2007, July). Towards a single development vision and the role of the single economy, presented at the Twenty-Eighth Meeting of the Conference of Heads of Government on the Caribbean Community, Needham's Point, Barbados.

Girvan, N. (2012, November). Colonialism and neo-colonialism in the Caribbean: An overview. Paper presented at the IV International Seminar Africa, the Caribbean, and Latin America, Kingston, Jamaica. Retrieved from www.normangirvan.info/wp-content/uploads/2013/01/Girvan-St-Vincent-paper.pdf

Grugel, J. (1995). *Politics and development in the Caribbean basin: Central America and the Caribbean in the new world order.* Bloomington, IN: Indiana University Press.

Harris, J. (2011, October). Word clouds considered harmful. Retrieved from www.labor.ucla.edu/wp-content/uploads/2015/03/word-clouds-harmful.pdf

International Monetary Fund (2005). Emigration and brain drain: Evidence from the Caribbean. Retrieved from www.imf.org/external/pubs/ft/wp/.../wp0625.pdf

International Monetary Fund (2012, April 12). World economic outlook: Western hemisphere, rebuilding strength and flexibility. Retrieved from www.imf.org/external/pubs/ft/reo/2012/whd/eng/pdf/wreo0412.pdf

Lincoln, Y. S., & Guba, E. G., (1985). *Naturalistic inquiry.* Newbury Park, CA: Sage.

McCabe, K. (2016, February). Report from The Migration Policy Institute. Retrieved from www.migrationpolicy.org

Memmi, A. (1956). *The colonizer and the colonized.* Boston, MA: Beacon Press.

Moustakas, C. (1994). *Phenomenological Research Methods.* London: Sage Publications.

Naipaul, V. (1969). *The Middle Passage.* New York, NY: Random House.

Olwig, K. F. (1985). *Cultural adaptation and resistance on St. John: Three centuries of Afro-Caribbean life.* Gainesville, FL: University Press of Florida.

Rodney, W. (1972). *How Europe underdeveloped Africa.* Baltimore, MD: Black Classic Press. (Original work published 1972).

Runco, M. (2014). *Creativity: Theories and themes: Research, development, and practice.* London: Academic Press.

Shepherd, V. (2011, March 28). Obstacles to the Creation of Afrocentric Societies in the Commonwealth Caribbean, Presentation Made to the WGPAD's 10th Session, March 28–April 1, 2011. Retrieved from: www.ohchr.org/Documents/Issues/Racism/WGEAPD/Session10/VShepherd.doc

Smith, L. (1999). *Decolonizing methodologies: Research and indigenous peoples.* New York, NY: St. Martin's Press.

Smith, J. A., & Eatough, V. (2007). Interpretative phenomenological analysis. In E. Lyons & A. Coyle (Eds), *Analysing qualitative data in psychology.* London: Sage, pp. 35–50.

Smith, J. A., Flowers, P., & Larkin, M. (2009). *Interpretative phenomenological analysis: Theory, method and research.* London: Sage.

Walcott, D. (2000). *Politics and poetics.* Gainesville, FL: University of Florida Press.

Williams, E. (1993). *Eric E. Williams speaks: Essays on Colonialism and Independence.* Wellesley, Massachusetts: Calaloux Publishing.

Yardley, L. (2008). Demonstrating validity in qualitative research. In J. A. Smith (Ed.) *Qualitative psychology: a practical guide to research methods,* London: Sage, pp. 235–251.

Zips, W. (2009). *Black rebels: African Caribbean freedom fighters in Jamaica.* Princeton, NJ: Markus Weiner.

Appendix A
Caribbean scholars

Césaire, Aimé

Born into poverty in Martinique in 1913, Césaire became a renowned scholar, poet, author, playwright, and politician (Heller, 2007). After earning academic scholarships to the Lycee Louis-le Grand, the Ecole Normale Superieure, and the Sorbonne in Paris, where he studied Latin, Greek, and French literature, he became one of the three founders of the *Negritude* movement (Davis, 1997). The other two founders, Leopold Senghor and Leon Damas, went on to become the first president of Senegal and a member of the French National Assembly respectively (Davis, 1997). The *Negritude* (blackness or negro-ness) movement, a term Césaire coined from the disparaging French term *negre*, was a resilient response to the idea that "Blacks" were a global equal (Nesbitt, 2014). The name alone represented the rejection of the European justification for slavery, which stated, "Africans were black because God had made them that way in order to announce their moral failure and their inferiority, these were ideas that helped Europeans live comfortable with the notion of slavery" (Higman, 2011, p. 79). The purpose of the *Negritude* movement was to reclaim an ill-conceived identity through the liberating instrument of literature, poetry, art, and political discourse for the unity of African peoples who historically suffered through the transatlantic slave trade (Davis, 1997). Césaire (1950) characterized the movement by stating, "Negritude is not a cephalic index, or plasma, or soma, but measured by the compass of suffering" (p. 125). His experiential reference to *suffering* seems to be a call to action, reclamation of ancestral roots, and the rejection of oppression. Influenced by Frobenius's position (Senghor, 1973) that, "the idea of the barbaric Negro was a European invention" (p. vii), Césaire's (1950) call to action included the reestablishment of the truest identity of black Africans living in the Caribbean.

Césaire used his "Disclosure on Colonialism" (1950) to condemn the European civilizations for the hundreds of years of oppression, expound on a parallel between Nazism and Colonialism, and reestablish the truest identity of the African people. He stated,

People are astounded, they are angry. They say: "How strange that is. But then it is only Nazism, it won't last." And they wait, and they hope; and they hide the truth from themselves: It is savagery, the supreme savagery, it crowns, it epitomizes the day-to-day savageries; yes, it is Nazism, but before they became its victims, they were its accomplices; that Nazism they tolerated before they succumbed to it, they exonerated it, they closed their eyes to it, they legitimated it because until then it had been employed only against non-European peoples; that Nazism they encouraged, they were responsible for it, and it drips, it seeps, it wells from every crack in western Christian civilization until it engulfs that civilization in a bloody sea.

(p. 36)

Disappointed in the efforts of the Martinique and French governments to improve the socioeconomic status in the Caribbean, Césaire refused to speak in Parliament throughout the 1950s (Nesbitt, 2014). Returning to teaching, he taught and mentored Frantz Fanon and Edouard Glissant, who would later become powerful voices of resistance in the Caribbean (Davis, 1997, p. 2). Césaire's significant works are, *Les Armes miraculeuses* (1946), *Et Les Chiens se taisaient* (1946), *Soleil cou-coupé* (1948), *Corps perdu* (1950), *Discourse on Colonialism* (1955), *Lettre á Maurice Thorez* (1956), *La Tragédie du roi Christophe* (1963), *Une Saison au Congo* (1966), *A Tempest* (1968), *A Notebook of the Return to my Native Land* (1947), and *The Collected Poetry* (1983).

Girvan, Norman

Born in Jamaica, Girvan's socioeconomic position was developed while completing his research for his PhD dissertation, "Rebellion, revolution, cultural affirmation and other forms of resistance are as integral to the Caribbean experience as are exploitation by external forces and internal elites" (Girvan, 2012). Rebellion, revolution, and cultural affirmation remained a core tenet of his research and writings throughout his career. Girvan later suggested that his research was inspired by a study group at the London School of Economics led by C. L. R. James and included Walter Rodney (Lewis, 1998). After earning his PhD in Economics, Girvan returned to his alma mater in Jamaica as a lifetime professor of Development and Economics at The University of the West Indies in Mona, Jamaica. While teaching at U.W.I. he authored an economic initiative that developed the CARICOM trade bloc (2007). The initiative dismantled the individual markets and established a single economy utilized by the majority of the Caribbean nations.

Girvan was appointed to positions of significant influence throughout his career: a member of the United Nations Committee on Development Policy for six years; the United Nations liaison between Guyana and Venezuela; director of the National Planning Agency in Jamaica; and the Secretary General of the Association of Caribbean States. Girvan's (1973) work, "The

Development of Dependency Economics in the Caribbean and Latin America: Review and comparison," significantly influenced the socio-economic processes throughout the decolonizing and neo-liberal periods.

Substantiating that he was a socioeconomic champion for all the cultures of the Caribbean, Girvan's final initiative was a campaign for the Haitian people scattered throughout the region. Seeking a change for the socio-economic state of the Haitian people, his last paper addressed the subject, "Denationalisation of Dominicans of Haitian descent" (Richards, 2013). Girvan recognized that the Haitian people were illegitimately bound to a state of oppression in their own land, which resulted in Haitian migration to other Caribbean islands. However, he concluded that the Haitian people arrived in their new destinations to more oppression.

James, C. L. R.

James was born in Trinidad and Tobago. His novel *Minty Alley* was the first novel published by a black Caribbean author in the United Kingdom (Paris, 1986). Known for his interdisciplinary aptitude, James authored significant works of Caribbean history, social justice, and cricket. Seeking to place the plight of the Africans in the Caribbean in an accurate historical context, James published *The Black Jacobins*, a historical account of the Haitian Revolution. Arguing that the Haitian Revolution was the only successful slave revolt in history (p. xi), James focused the work on the ideals of liberty and equality, which he believed "meant far more to them (as enslaved Haitians) than to any Frenchman" (p. 197).

The central figure in *The Black Jacobin* was Toussaint L'Ouverture, who rose to a position of freedom and power during the Haitian Revolution that began in 1791 (James, 2013). James seemed to recognize that the L'Ouverture character exceeded the image of a revolutionary figure and became "the apogee of the revolutionary doctrines that underpinned the French Revolution" (Lowe & Lloyd, 1997). James later used the plight of L'Ouverture as the basis for his three-act play, *Toussaint L'Ouverture: The Story of the Only Successful Slave Revolt in History*. James utilized the theatrical platform to convey a message of hope and freedom to his fellow Afro-Caribs throughout the Caribbean. He further expounded on his message in *Modern Politics:*

> The end toward which mankind is inexorably developing by the constant overcoming of internal antagonisms is not the enjoyment, ownership, or use of goods, but self-realization, creativity based upon the incorporation into the individual personality of the whole previous development of humanity. Freedom is creative universality, not utility.
>
> (James, 1960, p. 117)

Rosengarten (2008) further explained James's position of freedom: "James was scornful of the notion that black Afro-Caribs were a 'backward' and 'immature' people in need of benevolent guidance from the metropolitan center" (p. 12). James argued that education and intellectual life, "take their color and direction from those who have the power" (as cited in Rosengarten, 2008, p, 233). His position seems to be rooted in his life experience.

During his lifetime, positions of leadership throughout the Caribbean were appointed by colonial powers. James (1932) suggested in *The Life of Captain Cipriani*, "the masses cannot respect their own people when the highest positions are filled from abroad" (p. 12). As a result, James respectfully stood in opposition to the appointed leaders in his birth nation of Trinidad and Tobago, who seemed convinced that "colored people of the West Indian islands could not lead the respective nations" (as cited in Rosengarten, 2008, p. 233).

Despite his rejection of the leadership model throughout the region, James' (1938) respect for the discipline of the masses seemed constant—"When history is written as it ought to be written, it is the moderation and long patience of the masses at which men will wonder, not their ferocity" (p. 230). Although James marveled at the patience of the Afro-Carib people, his works reveal a man who was deeply burdened by 500 years of oppression. James' works are crucial to understanding the decolonization period and further serve to clarify the relationship between creative practice and socioeconomic crisis in the Caribbean.

Lewis, Arthur

Born in St. Lucia, Lewis was the recipient of the 1979 Noble Prize in Economics, became the first President of the Caribbean Development Bank, and was knighted for his contributions to economics (Nobel Media, 2014). Although Lewis taught at the University of Manchester for ten years, the University of the West Indies for four years, and Princeton University for nineteen years, his economic positions reached beyond the classroom. When the Republic of Ghana declared its autonomy in 1957, Lewis was asked to serve as its first economic advisor. As the author of the initial five-year development plan, Lewis's contributions positioned Ghana to become a global example of development. Now, the Institute of Economics and Peace (2013) considers Ghana the sixth largest economy in Africa and one of Africa's most developed countries. The indexes of stability, governance, and human development are ranked in the top three of Africa, while the country's GDP is considered one of the fastest growing in the world (Institute of Economics and Peace, 2013).

Lewis's works, "Economic Development with Unlimited Supplies of Labour" and *The Theory of Economic Growth* are significant sources that provide "an appropriate framework for studying economic development through curiosity and practical need" (Lewis, 1954, p. 139). His Duel Sector model has become known as the "Lewis Model," which has been implemented for growth by many scales of economy. China, the world's largest economic structure, acknowledges their economic development has been significantly influenced by the "Lewisian" turning point (Hamlin, 2010). Lewis's contributions to development economics and industrial structure have become a prevailing theory of transformational growth (Mookherjee, 2014).

Rodney, Walter

Born in British Guiana, which is the CARICOM nation of Guyana today, Rodney authored, *How Europe Underdeveloped Africa*, which is considered one of the foremost works on colonialism and its effects on the African people (Shivji, 2012). Rodney's works emphasized colonial oppression, the hardship of the poor, and the struggle endured by the working class Africans throughout the Caribbean. As a scholar and activists he was harshly critical of the middle class in the Caribbean for their role in the decolonization and development eras (Bogues, 2009). He felt that the middle class secured their cultural position through the labor of the poor, which was only a slight variation from the imperialistic model. Rodney held to the position that the African communities throughout the world should focus on fluid harmonization and unity among themselves (Young, 2008).

When Rodney arrived in Kingston, Jamaica in 1968 to teach at his alma mater, The University of the West Indies, he seemed determined to increase the political and cultural consciousness among the poor (Ledgister & Waters, 2008). Convinced by Jamaican intelligence officers that Rodney was a threat to national security on the island, Prime Minister Hugh Shearer issued a *persona non grata*, which banned Rodney from ever returning to the island nation (USNA, 1968). Justifying his actions, Shearer stated, "Never in the history of modern Jamaica has there been a man who provided greater threat to the security of Jamaica than Rodney" (USNA, 1968).

Since Rodney was attending a writer's conference in Montreal when the *persona non grata* was issued, the Jamaican government denied him from clearing immigration in the Montreal airport, which prohibited him from returning to the island. Being exiled in Canada, Rodney quickly wrote a rebuttal to the Jamaican government, "The Jamaican government has a large percentage of Black Men, but as the brothers say, they are 'white hearted,' traitors to the Black Race, and have no moral authority to lay accusations against me, a son of Africa" (Rodney, 1969, p. 4). Taking into account the intelligence provided by the Jamaican government and Rodney's manifesto of rebuttal, the Canadian government followed suit and banned Rodney from their country.

Started by students at The University of the West Indies, his banishments were the catalysts of riots throughout Kingston (Ledgister & Waters, 2008). Although the riots only lasted several days, the residual effect of the rebellion "brought the question of fundamental social and economic change to the centre of the political stage in Jamaica" (Payne, 1995, p. 158). The riots, called the Rodney Riots, later inspired the mutiny of the police on Trinidad and Tobago and further accentuated Rodney's call for socioeconomic change throughout the region.

Rodney's contribution to Caribbean history is his relentless commitment to promote African political autonomy and economic wellbeing in the Caribbean and Africa (Young, 2008). The majority of his work was aimed at the working class African peoples in the Caribbean, along with Africa, and Guyana. His revolutionary thinking helped shape a socioeconomic discourse in the decolonization period of Caribbean history.

Walcott, Derek

Born in St. Lucia, his influence on Caribbean literature is reflected in the numerous global awards he has received: 1992 Nobel Prize for Literature, 1981 MacArthur Foundation "Genius" award, 1971 Obie Award, 1988 Queen's Medal for Poetry, 1966 Royal Society of Literature Award, 2011 T. S. Eliot Prize, and 2011 OCM Bocas Prize for Caribbean Literature, among others. The Nobel Prize Committee characterized his work as, "a poetic oeuvre of great luminosity, sustained by a historical vision, the outcome of a multicultural commitment" (Nobel Foundation, 2007, p. 191). Living through four historical periods in the Caribbean—colonization, decolonizing, development, and neo-liberal periods—Walcott used the reality of Afro-Carib life as his perspective for the majority of his works. Although Walcott often referenced the residual damage to the region from colonialism, slavery, and oppression (i.e., *Dream on Monkey Mountain* and *Omeros*), he seemed committed in developing the broad possibilities of the future rather than dwelling on the atrocities of the past. This idea is clearly identified in an interview, *The Art of Poetry No. 37*, which he stated,

> If we continue to sulk and say, Look at what the slave owner did, and so forth, we will never mature. While we sit moping or writing morose poems and novels that glorify a non-existent past, then time passes us by.
>
> (Hirsch & Walcott, 1986, p. 101)

Walcott feared that the African cultures of the Caribbean would be snared in the oppressive and fragmented images of the past. His concern for the region's identity remains a constant theme in his works.

Passionate about his Christian faith, Walcott believed that his message of hope for the African cultures was the result of God's inspiration on his poetry. Walcott stated, "I have never separated the writing of poetry from prayer. I have grown up believing it is a vocation, a religious vocation" (Walcott, 1986). Walcott's themes of hope and unity through the free expression of arts help to clarify the relationship between creativity and the socioeconomic crisis in the Caribbean.

References

Bogues, A. (2009). Black power, decolonization, and Caribbean politics: Walter Rodney and the politics of 'the groundings with my brothers'. *Boundary 2*, 36(1): 127–147.

Césaire, A. (1950). *Discourse on colonialism.* New York, NY: Monthly Review Press.

Davis, D. (1997). *Routes to slavery: direction, ethnicity and morality in the transatlantic slave trade.* Portland, OR: Frank Cass.

Girvan, N. (2007, July). Towards a single development vision and the role of the single economy, presented at the Twenty-Eighth Meeting of the Conference of Heads of Government on the Caribbean Community, Needham's Point, Barbados.

Girvan, N. (2012, November). Colonialism and neo-colonialism in the Caribbean: An overview. Paper presented at the IV International Seminar Africa, the Caribbean, and Latin America, Kingston, Jamaica. Retrieved from www.normangirvan.info/wp-content/uploads/2013/01/Girvan-St-Vincent-paper.pdf

Girvan, N., & Girvan C. (1973). The development of dependency economics in the Caribbean and Latin America: Review and comparison. *Social and Economic Studies*, 22(1): 1–33. Retrieved from http://sesjournaluwi.blogspot.com

Hamlin, K. (2010, June 11). China reaches turning point as inflation overtakes labor. *Bloomberg.* Retrieved from www.bloomberg.com/apps/news?pid=newsarchive&sid=aZGJ0mc_Dm5o.

Heller, B. A. (2007). Césaire, Aimé. In D. Balderston & M. Gonzalez (Eds), *Encyclopedia of Latin American and Caribbean Literature, 1900–2003,* New York, NY: Routledge, pp. 128–130.

Higman, B. (2011). *A concise history of the Caribbean.* New York, NY: Cambridge Press.

Hirsch, E., & Walcott, D. (1986). Interviews: Derek Walcott, the art of poetry no. 37. *The Paris Review*, 101. Retrieved from www.theparisreview.org

Institute of Economics and Peace (2013). Measuring the state of global peace. Retrieved from www.visionofhumanity.org/pdf/gpi/2013_Global_Peace_Index_Report.pdf

James, C. L. R. (1932). *The life of Captain Cipriani: An account of British government in the West Indies.* Port of Spain, Trinidad & Tobago: Nelson, Lancs, Cartmel & Co.

James, C. L. R. (1938). *The black jacobins.* London: Secker & Warburg.

James, C. L. R. (1960). *Modern politics.* Port of Spain, Trinidad & Tobago: PNM Publishing.

James, C. L. R. (1983). *At the rendezvous of victory.* London: Allison & Busby.

James, C. L. R. (2013). Toussaint L'Ouverture: The story of the only successful slave revolt in history; a play in three acts. (C. Hogsbjerg, Ed.). Durham, NC: Duke University Press. (Original work published 1934).

Ledgister, F., & Waters, A. (2008). Public scholarship and political action: The memory of Walter Rodney in Jamaica. *Wadabagei*, 11(1): 4–35. Retrieved from www.academia.edu/2190326/Public_Scholarship_and_Political_Action_The_Memory_of_Walter_Rodney_in_Jamaica

Lewis, A. (1950). The industrialization of the British West Indies. *Caribbean Economic Review*, 5(50).

Lewis, A. (1954). Economic theories of development: an analysis of competing paradigms. New York, NY: Harvester Wheatsheaf.

Lewis, R. (1998). *Walter Rodney's intellectual and political thought.* Kingston, Jamaica. The Press University of the West Indies.

Lowe, L., & Lloyd, D. (1997). *The politics of culture in the shadow of capital*. Durham, NC: Duke University Press.

Mookherjee, D. (2014, October). Development and structural transformation: the Lewis model. Lecture 9–10, Boston University, September 30 and October 2, 2014.

Nesbitt, N. (2014, May 30). From Louverture to Lenin: Aimé Césaire and the problem of the postcolonial state. Paper presented at Rethinking Césaire Conference, University of California, Santa Barbara. Retrieved from www.academia.edu/7218177/From_Louverture_to_Lenin_Aimé_Césaire_and_the_Problem_of_the_Postcolonial_State

Nobel Foundation, (2007). *Nobel lectures: From the literature laureates, 1986 to 2006.* Melbourne, Melbourne University Press.

Nobel Media AB. (2014). The Sveriges Riksbank prize in economic sciences in memory of Alfred Nobel 1979. *Nobelprize.org.* Retrieved from www.nobelprize.org/nobel_prizes/economics/laureates/1979/

Paris, D. (1986). *C. L. R. James: His life and work.* London: Allison & Busby.

Payne, A. (1995). *Politics in Jamaica.* New York, NY: St. Martin's Press.

Richards, P. (2013, November). CARICOM defers Dominican Republic application amid row over court ruling. Retrieved from www.caribbean360.com/news/trinidad_tobago_news/caricom-defers-dominican-republic-application-amid-row-over-court-ruling

Rodney, W. (1969). *The groundings of my brothers.* London: Bogle-L'Ouverture Publications.

Rodney, W. (1972). *How Europe underdeveloped Africa.* Baltimore, MD: Black Classic Press. (Original work published 1972).

Rosengarten, F. (2008). *Urbane revolutionary: C. L. R. James and the struggle for a new society.* Oxford, MS: The University of Mississippi Press.

Senghor, L. (1973). The Lessons of Leo Frobenius, in E. Haberland (Ed.), *Leo Frobenius: An Anthology,* (Wiesbaden: Franz Steiner Verlag), p. vii; Jacqueline Leiner, "Entretien avec A.C."

Shivji, I. G. (2012, December). Remembering Walter Rodney. *Monthly Review,* 64(7). Retrieved from http://monthlyreview.org

UNSA, file Pol. 21: Amembassy Kingston to Department of State, October 18, 1968.

Walcott, D. (1969) *The Gulf.* New York, NY: Macmillan Press.

Walcott, D. (1970) *Dream on Monkey Island.* New York, NY: Macmillan Press.

Walcott, D. (1984) *Midsummer: XXVII.* New York, NY: Macmillan Press.

Walcott, D. (2000). *Politics and poetics.* Gainesville, FL: University of Florida Press.

Young, K. B. (2008). Walter Rodney's Pan-African nationalism. *Peace Review,* 20(4): 487–495. DOI:10.1080/10402650802495106.

Appendix B
Attributes of a systems view of life

A systems view of life considers the whole planet as a living, self-regulating system, where creativity is the driving force of the self-generation (Capra & Luisi, 2014). A high priority challenge for the Caribbean, which is grounded in hundreds of years of socioeconomic crisis, is to create and nurture sustainable communities, not construct economic growth or advantage. A sustainable community is designed such that its ways of life, businesses, economy, physical structures, and qualities reflect an organic ability to sustain life (Capra & Luisi, 2014). According to a systems view, communities are understood as a whole rather than as a collection of parts (Capra & Luisi, 2014). That is, all essential properties within the *whole* are defined by and depend on relationships; whereas, the *parts* are defined as isolated objects. Capra (2014) further clarifies this approach to living systems need when he suggested, "Understanding life requires a shift of focus from objects to relationships" (p. 83). A practical example of this shift in focus can be seen in the CARICOM, which collectively represents the Caribbean Community as a group of Caribbean nations committed to the whole region, holistically. The central objective for CARICOM is to "improve the standards of living and work" through a unified approach (Caribbean Community Secretariat, 2013). For instance, twenty-one nations in the Caribbean form a collective union for trade, assist one another with sustainable economic development, and elevate the region's competitive advantage (Caribbean Community Secretariat, 2013). At the same time, the United States Virgin Islands are not members of CARICOM. They have chosen to remain an isolated object, which has further deepened their dependence on the United States and elevated their socioeconomic crisis.

When a system fails to attend to the collective whole, it views and responds to growth and crisis with linear and isolating concepts. Capra and Luisi (2014) suggest that understanding crisis begins with understanding the phenomenon of isolation. Crisis can occur within many components of life and pertain to energy, food, ecology, climate, and financial security; these components, and the crisis that may affect them, cannot be completely understood in isolation. Attempting to solve a crisis by concentrating exclusively on an individual component of a living system, such as the economy, is a horizontal perspective of crisis that will ultimately create higher levels of chaos (Capra & Luisi, 2014). Capra (2002) suggested that no living system can survive in isolation and "nothing is meaningful in itself" (pp. 84–85). When a crisis occurs in a living system, that hardship connects to and depends upon, all aspects of the living system (Capra & Luisi, 2014). In an economic context, a key challenge posed by systems theory necessitates shifting perspectives from one involving isolated effort toward economic growth to one that is sustainable and socially just (Capra & Luisi: 2014). In the Caribbean, focus on economic growth for 500 years seems to have resulted in escalating injustice, increased isolation, and further economic hardship.

Although some hypothesize that no growth or negative should be a global objective, Capra and Luisi (2014) have argued, "growth is an essential characteristic to all life" (p. 368). Growth in nature is neither linear nor unlimited; rather, it is qualitative. Lappe (2009) suggested that most of what we understand to be growth today is waste; however, qualitative growth seeks to enhance the quality of life through generation and regeneration. Acknowledging that the residents of the Caribbean continue to suffer through significant poverty, the highest debt ratios in the world, and crime rates that seem insurmountable, it seems reasonable that the residents of the Caribbean would question their quality of life and reach for qualitative growth. Without recourse to creating or recreating for themselves, Caribbean countries and colonies continue to rely on other cultures for innovation and change, thus accepting a hegemonic agenda that ultimately perpetuates crisis and chaos. Further, socioeconomic dependency jeopardizes the future of the dependent culture and suppresses its truest identity through the socioeconomic objectives of the hegemonic nations.

In light of the region's long-term dependency on imperialistic/hegemonic nations, this research considers whether Caribbean crisis and chaos have resulted from outsourcing the abilities to create and recreate. Capra and Luisi (2014) suggested,

> A systemic understanding of life sheds new light on the ago-old philosophical debate about freedom and determinism. The key point is that the behavior of a living organism is constrained but not determined by outside forcers. Living organisms are self-organizing, meaning that their behavior is not imposed by the environment but is established by the system itself. More specifically, the organism's behavior is determined by its own structure, a structure formed by a succession of autonomous structural changes.
>
> (p. 309)

Based on Capra and Luisi's (2014) living systems view of life, freedom is defined by the behavior of the living organism (p. 309). In the context of the Caribbean, the organism could be characterized as the *periphery*, while the outside forces are the defined as the *center*. Although the organism called the *periphery* may be constrained by the outside forces of the center, living organisms should be self-organizing. However, if the behavioral patterns of the *periphery* are organized as a dysfunctional structure, then the structural changes could also produce dysfunctional outcomes.

Based on the position of Capra and Luisi (2014), if the freedom to create or re-create is suppressed or destroyed, then the living system could become unstable, dysfunctional, and die in isolation (2014, p. 130). Therefore, it seems imperative for the functionality, identity, meaning, and freedom of the Caribbean that the region reestablishes the ability to create and recreate.

To satisfy the objectives of my research, I have utilized scholars from diverse disciplines, analyzed the evolution of the socioeconomic crisis in the Caribbean, and illuminated the reality of life in the Caribbean from the onset. The historical progression, coupled with validated theoretical positions, support the reality of a socioeconomic crisis that is bordering on region wide catastrophe. In addition, I have suggested that the current hardship experienced in the everyday lives of residents may be the result of an omission or suppression of a key component in the *initial conditions* of the region, which has thwarted development and independence for 500 years. Based on multidisciplinary scholarship and comprehensive research that spans five centuries, I recognize that creativity was strategically omitted in the formation of development and independence for the Caribbean. In what follows, I rehearse theories, ideas and observations from respected scholars that support the necessity of creativity as a sustainable function of life. This scholarship substantiates the notion that living systems, like culture(s), require conscious creativity, while the absence or suppression of creativity in the *initial conditions* has a chaotic effect (Capra, 2014; Runco, 2014).

References

Capra, F. (2002). *The hidden connections: Integrating the biological, cognitive, and social dimensions of life into a science of sustainability.* New York, NY: Doubleday.

Capra, F., & Luisi, P. (2014). *The systems view of life: A unifying vision.* Cambridge, England: Cambridge Press.

Caribbean Community Secretariat. (2013, February). Caribbean community: Regional aid for trade strategy 2013–2015. *CARICOM.* Retrieved from www.caricom.org/Caribbean_Community_AfT_Strategy_final.pdf

Lappe, F., (2011). *Ecomind: Changing the way we think, to create the world we want.* New York, NY: Nation Books.

Runco, M. (2014). *Creativity: Theories and themes: Research, development, and practice.* London: Academic Press.

Glossary A
Academic terms

1 **Accumulation** A process of capitalism where commodities are sold, then the money is converted to capital.

2 **Adaptive cycle** Nations and/or cultures historically progress through periods of stability, challenge, crisis and reorganization; however, based on the decisions of leadership, the progression can stall on any one the stages. The cycle can serve as an assessment tool of progress. For the purpose of this paper, the Caribbean has been stalled in the crisis phase for many decades.

3 **Afro-Caribs** Africans in the Caribbean. Africans were violently displaced from their indigenous homelands and relocated via the Trans-Atlantic slave trade to the Caribbean.

4 **Bauxite** A small rock-like mineral. The world's largest source of aluminum. Bauxite is primarily found in wet tropical environments, such as Jamaica.

5 **Caribbean** The islands, sea, and coastlines within the region north of South America, South and Southeast of the United States. The population in the Caribbean exceeds forty million people.

6 **CARICOM** Caribbean Community (formerly known as CARIFTA (Caribbean Free Trade Association). Through the establishment of CARICOM, the region formed a common market with agreed upon objectives. The fifteen members, which are Antigua and Barbuda, Bahamas, Barbados, Belize, Dominica, Haiti, Jamaica, Grenada, Guyana, Montserrat, St. Lucia, Suriname, St. Kitts and Nevis, St. Vincent and the Grenadines, and Trinidad and Tobago, have combined to form economic leverage to enhance the lives of their residents.

7 **Chaos** Patterns of behavior that develop from established conditions. For the purpose of this project, chaos in the nations of the Caribbean seems to be the result of the initial conditions that the imperial nations established in the region.

8 **Core** Prebisch (1951) suggested that the industrialized core, what many economists call the *center*, was a position of hegemony for the purpose of exploiting the prices of agriculture and raw materials from underdeveloped nations, which are also called the *periphery*. For the purpose of this project, the core is primarily the industrialized European Community. The periphery is the Caribbean.

9 **Creativity** An essential component of self-generation and improvement. As Runco (2014) stated, "Creativity is a vital form of human capital.... Creativity both contributes to the information explosion and helps us cope and adapt to the resulting challenges ... creativity is partly intentional, partly a matter of choice" (2014, p. xi). For the purpose of this project, creativity is an essential component for defusing the socio-economic crisis in the Caribbean.

10 **Crisis** When the coping mechanism within a living system becomes dysfunctional and threatens to destabilize the entire system, a crisis develops. For the purpose of the project, the coping mechanism within the living system called the Caribbean became dysfunctional and destabilized the entire region.

11 **Decolonization** A strategic process of independence from a imperialistic/colonial position. The process includes the establishment of economic, social and political structures. For the purpose of this project, the islands of the Caribbean decolonized from the European Community.

12 **Dependency** According to Chilcote, when a nation is unable to accumulate and expand capital, the result is dependency on dominant countries that can expand capital and be self-sustaining. For the purpose of this paper, the countries of the Caribbean have been dependent on domain countries in the European Community, the United States, and Canada (1984, p. 164).

13 **Development of Underdevelopment** Development is generated in an industrialized core through a strategic stagnation of development in a peripheral region/country. For the purpose of this project, the European Community strategically developed their respective nations through a stagnation or oppression in the islands of the Caribbean.

14 **Favored status** A reference to the preferential access established in the Lome Agreement.

15 **Hegemony** A position of dominance, which includes economic, social, ideological, and cultural influence. For the purpose of this project, the European Community established a position of hegemony over the Caribbean.

16 **Horizontal Analysis** Due to the hardship associated with crisis, there seems to be a tendency to attempt to rectify crisis based on their current

state of being; however, there are legitimate factors that caused the crisis. A horizontal analysis only views the crisis in its current state, while omitting the conditions in the original form that constructed to the crisis.

17 **Living Systems**   Capra and Luisi (2014) proposed living systems as a system view of life, "A view of the world as an integrated whole rather than a disassociated collection of parts" (p. xi). They further define living systems as a conception of life that includes, "relationships, patterns, and context" (p. 12).

18 **Lome Agreement**   The agreement has evolved through four revisions. Originally signed in 1975, the European Community agreed with the African, Caribbean, and Pacific states to allow duty free agriculture and minerals into the European Community. The agreement also established preferential access to European markets and fixed prices on sugar, fruit, and other agricultural products.

19 **Manufactured culture**   I developed the designation to accurately describe imperialistic actions that extracted cultures from their indigenous countries and place them against their will in foreign lands for the sole purpose of economic advantage. For the purpose of this project, the reference point is the Afro-Carib/West Indian culture. Although the Afro-Carib/West Indian culture has been in the Caribbean for over 500 years, it is not indigenous to the Caribbean.

20 **Periphery**   A country or region that is not able, through a position of hegemony, to accumulate capital or reproduce itself. The land, minerals, and agriculture are exploited for the purpose of developing an industrialized core. For the purpose of this project, the periphery is comprised of the nations of the Caribbean. The core is primarily the industrialized European Community.

21 **Region**   For the purpose of this project, the term encompasses the entire Caribbean.

22 **Resilience**   For the purpose of this project, the capacity of the nations in the Caribbean to recover from longstanding crisis.

23 **Unequal exchange**   A strategic structure of international trade. The industrialized core or developing country exchanges commodities that are of different kinds with a underdeveloped country for the purpose of development/underdevelopment. The commodities represent forms of wealth.

24 **West Indian**   The West Indies (commonly known as the Caribbean) is a cumulative designation for the islands within the Greater Antilles, Lesser Antilles, and the Bahamas. The people with an African ontology are defined as West Indians. However, the term West Indian resulted from Columbus' error. When he landed in the Caribbean, he thought was actually in the East Indies (Asia). When the mistake was realized, the term West Indies (West Indians) was used to describe the region and its people.

References

Capra, F., & Luisi, P. (2014). *The systems view of life: A unifying vision.* Cambridge, England: Cambridge Press.

Chilcote, R. (1984). *Theories of development and underdevelopment.* Boulder, CO: Westview Press.

Prebisch, R. (1951). Growth, disequilibrium and disparities: Interpretation of the process of economic development. *Economic survey of Latin America 1949.* Santiago, Chile: ECLAC.

Runco, M. (2014). *Creativity: Theories and themes: Research, development, and practice.* London: Academic Press.

Glossary B
Culture specific terms

1 **Boi**   An Afro-Carib term for friend; i.e., "Me boi, watch yourself."

2 **Deh**   An Afro-Carib term that replaces the English term "the"; i.e., "Deh game is on."

3 **Ganja**   Cultural term for Marijuana, which the Rastafarians believe is a source of spiritual enlightenment.

4 **Herb**   Cultural term for Marijuana, which the Rastafarians believe is a source of spiritual enlightenment.

5 **Johnny Cakes**   A common Afro-Carib food found through the region: fried corn meal mixed with water, milk, and a spice of choice.

6 **Mehson**   An Afro-Carib term for friend; i.e., "Watch yourself mehson."

7 **Patois**   Vernacular form of English spoken throughout the Caribbean; however, Afro-Caribs have developed the terminology and dialect throughout many decades. Patois is a defining and rich component of communication within the Afro-Carib culture.

8 **Rastafarian**   Followers of Rastafarianism, which could be considered a liberation faith. The followers believe that Haile Selassie, the former Emperor of Ethiopia, was the reincarnated Savior and that all oppressed Africans will be liberated from their oppressors.

9 **Rastaman**   A man who follows the Rastafarian philosophy, usually identified by dreadlocks.

10 **Ting**   A grapefruit based drink that some consider to be the drink of the Caribbean.

Index

Page numbers in *italics* denote tables, those in **bold** denote figures.

mobility, and migration 113
Modern Politics 135
Morgan, A. 94
Morgan, K. 35
Mount, G. 53
Moustakas, C. 104

Naiman, L. 73
Naipaul, V.S. 62, 66, 67
Nazism 133–4
Negritude movement 133
Negus, K. 73–4, 81
neoliberal model 41, 44
neoliberal period 41–5, 46;
    contemporary relevance 44–5;
    exploitation 44
Neuman, W. 93
Newton, R. 96
Nine Mile 23–5
Norton, B. 77
NVivo software 102

Olwig, K.F. 60, 67, 92
oneness 110–11; resilience in oneness
    110
ontology 93–4; oneness 110–11
opportunity deprivation 26–9
opportunity, and migration 113
oppression, and anger 61
Ormrod, J. 94
outcomes: of creativity 74–5; of cultural
    conditioning 60–1; of intimidating
    power 53–4; of underdevelopment
    56–7
Oviedo 35

Palmie, S. 35, 36
Panarchy adaptive cycle 76–7
paradise, Caribbean as 30
Parajuli, P. 99
Pascal, B. 54
patriotism 126
patterns of relationship 64
Patton, M.Q. 96, 99
Payne, A. 137
personal growth 125–6
phenomenology 95–6
Pickering, M. 73–4, 81
place: sense of 79–80; transforming 71
plantation economy, creation of 35
planting a garden 18–22
Poincaré, H. 63, 65
population decline 32–4
positionality, author 3, 9–10, 50

potential: realization of 118; transforming
    71; unleashing 71–2
poverty: colonialism 36; neoliberal
    period 44; unemployment and
    migration 113
power: intimidating 52–4
practice, defining 6
Prebisch, R. 52–3, 54, 55, 56
Prescott College 107, 110
profit center perspective 32
profit center theory *83*
profit centers: establishment of 33, 35;
    extraction of wealth 36
public sector, development of 40
purposeful sampling 96

qualitative growth 142
qualitative method 93–5
qualitative research projects *96*
quantitative approach 93

Randall, S. 53
Rastafarian, encounter with 17–18
reader expectations *6*
"Rebellion, revolution, cultural
    affirmation and other forms of
    resistance are as integral to the
    Caribbean experience as are
    exploitation by external forces and
    internal elites" 134
regeneration for sustainable growth 74
Rehorick, D. 95
relational culture 3
research conclusions 122–9;
    bi-directional relationship 122;
    contingencies for socioeconomic
    growth 122; creative practice 125–6;
    expanded reality 123; intentionality
    123–4; migration 124–5
research design/objective **5**
research design: overview 4
research expectations *6*
research findings: awareness 108–9;
    cohesive family units 110–11; context
    and overview 108; corroboration of
    meaning 114, 116; creativity as innate
    and essential 118–22; credibility
    108–9; cultural value of creativity
    116–18; direct quotation 108;
    disconfirmation 109; individual and
    cultural growth 113–15; personal
    growth 125–6; resilience in oneness
    110; sense of place 111–13; SPEC
    question *110*; synthesized words of

Taylor & Francis eBooks

Helping you to choose the right eBooks for your Library

Add Routledge titles to your library's digital collection today. Taylor and Francis ebooks contains over 50,000 titles in the Humanities, Social Sciences, Behavioural Sciences, Built Environment and Law.

Choose from a range of subject packages or create your own!

Benefits for you

» Free MARC records
» COUNTER-compliant usage statistics
» Flexible purchase and pricing options
» All titles DRM-free.

Benefits for your user

» Off-site, anytime access via Athens or referring URL
» Print or copy pages or chapters
» Full content search
» Bookmark, highlight and annotate text
» Access to thousands of pages of quality research at the click of a button.

| REQUEST YOUR **FREE** INSTITUTIONAL TRIAL TODAY | **Free Trials Available** We offer free trials to qualifying academic, corporate and government customers. |

eCollections – Choose from over 30 subject eCollections, including:

Archaeology	Language Learning
Architecture	Law
Asian Studies	Literature
Business & Management	Media & Communication
Classical Studies	Middle East Studies
Construction	Music
Creative & Media Arts	Philosophy
Criminology & Criminal Justice	Planning
Economics	Politics
Education	Psychology & Mental Health
Energy	Religion
Engineering	Security
English Language & Linguistics	Social Work
Environment & Sustainability	Sociology
Geography	Sport
Health Studies	Theatre & Performance
History	Tourism, Hospitality & Events

For more information, pricing enquiries or to order a free trial, please contact your local sales team:
www.tandfebooks.com/page/sales

 Routledge
Taylor & Francis Group

The home of Routledge books

www.tandfebooks.com

For Product Safety Concerns and Information please contact our EU representative GPSR@taylorandfrancis.com Taylor & Francis Verlag GmbH, Kaufingerstraße 24, 80331 München, Germany